# The Mail ON SUNDAY

# PUB Quiz BOOK

D0892745

Chambers

CHAMBERS
An imprint of Chambers Harrap Publishers Ltd
7 Hopetoun Crescent
Edinburgh
EH7 4AY

www.chambers.co.uk

First published by Chambers Harrap Publishers Ltd 2007

A CIP catalogue record for this book is available from the British Library.

ISBN 978 0550 10348 2

**FSC**
**Mixed Sources**
Product group from well-managed
forests and other controlled sources

Cert no. SGS - COC - 2061
www.fsc.org
© 1996 Forest Stewardship Council

Designed and typeset by Chambers Harrap Publishers Ltd, Edinburgh
Printed in Great Britain by Clays Ltd, St Ives plc

# CONTENTS

# CONTRIBUTORS

## THE MAIL ON SUNDAY PUB QUIZ COMPILER

John Feetenby

## THE MAIL ON SUNDAY PUZZLE MEISTER

Chris Feetenby

## CHAMBERS EDITOR

Hazel Norris

## EDITORIAL ASSISTANCE

Vicky Aldus

Kate Amann

Katie Brooks

Francine Toon

## PREPRESS

Andrew Butterworth

Helen Hucker

Heather Macpherson

Becky Pickard

# INTRODUCTION

## BY JOHN FEETENBY

Whenever I tell someone that I compile *The Mail on Sunday* pub quiz, and embarrassingly I do this quite a lot, their response tends to go along the same lines. 'Wow, that's interesting,' they say. Then, after a moment or two of thinking about it, they continue, 'Of course, it must be quite easy. You just ask a bunch of questions and then Bob's your uncle.'

At this point I think two things. The first is something like, 'Crikey. Bob's your uncle. There's an interesting phrase. I wonder where it comes from. I wonder if there's a quiz question to be had out of it.'

The second is, 'You only think it's easy because you've never tried it, mate.' There are all sorts of pitfalls. A question that seems a great idea when you write it, for example, might be hideously inappropriate by the time it comes to be published, months down the line. Celebrities almost never consider the poor quiz compiler before embarking on a debauched murder spree.

Also, you have to be absolutely scrupulously accurate about sourcing everything, even the stuff you think you know. There is always somebody out there who knows more than you do.

And finally, you have to ask the question unambiguously, so that any answer given is definitely right or definitely wrong.

I can illustrate this by telling you about what befell three friends of mine, whom we shall call Lawrence, Toby and James to protect the innocent. Together they had entered a real pub quiz, and by real I mean it took place in an actual pub, not over the family breakfast table on a relaxed Sunday morning. Possibly drink had been taken, I don't know. I wasn't there.

At any rate, as we join the action they are doing quite well, hurtling towards the prize ahead of most of the field but neck and neck with the despised Purple Cobras. Then up comes the final round: true or false. Our guys can feel their hands on the trophy, or at least they can until the deciding question is read out thus:

'Sir Walter Raleigh's *window* carried his severed head around with her after his execution. True or false.'

Some vigorous, fiercely whispered debate follows. His *widow* almost certainly did, but that's not the question. The question is about his *window*, which can't have carried his head around. Windows can't carry stuff. It's a trick, they decide.

FALSE!

Of course, they were wrong. It wasn't a trick question, just one that hadn't been proofread properly.

The appeals procedure was disappointing to say the least. 'It says *window* on the card,' they were told, and that was it. Fortune and glory and maybe even free beer eluded them, and all because of a faulty question set by a quiz compiler who didn't check his or her work. Years later my friends are still vastly indignant about it.

I hope you enjoy the questions that follow. They span almost five years of publication, and were written to cover a broad range of subjects and a wide spectrum of difficulty. Don't worry if you get nowhere near ten out of ten on each of them. In fact, it would be worrying if you did. But do applaud yourself for every one you do get right. Knowledge is to be celebrated.

We live in times when finding anything out is as easy as double-clicking a mouse button, but there is a particular satisfaction to finding the information in your own head. And it's a lot cheaper than broadband.

Good luck.

*John Feetenby*
*The Mail on Sunday Pub Quiz compiler*
*Inverness, April 2007*

# QUIZZES

# QUIZ 1

**1 MOVIES**
Which was the fourth James Bond film to be released?

**2 MUSIC**
What instrument was played by the jazz musician Thelonious Monk?

**3 TV AND RADIO**
Which village is situated near Trumpton and Camberwick Green?

**4 SPORT AND LEISURE**
Who was the first Australian cricketer to be knighted?

**5 HISTORY**
Who was the British prime minister at the outbreak of World War I?

**6 GEOGRAPHY**
Which river runs through York?

**7 LITERATURE**
What is unique about the book *A Void* by Georges Perec?

**8 SCIENCE AND NATURE**
Diamonds are a form of which chemical element?

**9 WORDS**
What is an 'amanuensis'?
- a) a piece of music
- b) a literary assistant
- c) a knee swelling

**10 POT LUCK**
Where would you find a lych gate?

ANSWERS ON PAGE 255

# QUIZ 2

**1   MOVIES**
Which musical film in 2000 teamed singer Björk with actress Catherine Deneuve?

**2   MUSIC**
As well as performing vocals, which instrument did Phil Collins play in Genesis?

**3   TV AND RADIO**
Which long-running drama was set in St Angela's Hospital in Battersea?

**4   SPORT AND LEISURE**
What has been the nickname of two famous US boxers, one with the surname Robinson and the other Leonard?

**5   HISTORY**
In 1946, in which country did Enver Hoxha depose King Zog?

**6   SCIENCE AND NATURE**
Henry Deringer was an early US manufacturer of which products?

**7   LITERATURE**
Which literary bear was created by Michael Bond?

**8   CELEBRITIES**
What was Larry David's post-*Seinfeld* sitcom called?

**9   WORDS**
What does 'pulchritude' mean?
    a) beauty
    b) plainness
    c) ugliness

**10   POT LUCK**
Which musician was the subject of Martin Scorsese's documentary *No Direction Home*?

ANSWERS ON PAGE 255

# QUIZ 3

**1 MOVIES**
For which film did Gwyneth Paltrow win the Best Actress Oscar in 1998?

**2 MUSIC**
With which country is mariachi music associated?

**3 TV AND RADIO**
What was the first programme shown on Channel 4 at its launch in 1982?

**4 SPORT AND LEISURE**
Which British football team plays at Craven Cottage?

**5 HISTORY**
Which war was waged between 1861 and 1865?

**6 GEOGRAPHY**
What is the capital city of Canada?

**7 LITERATURE**
In Charles Dickens's novel *A Tale of Two Cities*, which cities was he writing about?

**8 SCIENCE AND NATURE**
Who was the second man on the Moon?

**9 WORDS**
What is a 'tabard'?
        a) a drum
        b) a bird
        c) an item of clothing

**10 POT LUCK**
How deep is a fathom?

ANSWERS ON PAGE 255

# QUIZ 4

**1 MOVIES**

In which Bond movie did Britt Ekland play Mary Goodnight?

**2 MUSIC**

Which jazz trumpeter recorded the legendary album *Kind of Blue* in 1959?

**3 TV AND RADIO**

In *Mary, Mungo and Midge*, what kind of animal was Mungo?

**4 SPORT AND LEISURE**

In tennis, what is the term given to winning the Australian Open, the French Open, the US Open and Wimbledon in the same calendar year?

**5 HISTORY**

Who led the Nationalists in the Spanish civil war in the 1930s?

**6 SCIENCE AND NATURE**

Where in the body would you find the 'corpus callosum' and the 'hippocampus'?

**7 LITERATURE**

David Peace's 2006 novel *The Damned United* was about which larger-than-life football manager?

**8 CELEBRITIES**

In which Jim Carrey movie does Kate Winslet play Clementine, a character who has had all memories of their relationship surgically removed?

**9 WORDS**

To what is an organism responding in the process of 'heliotaxis'?

  a) sunlight
  b) sudden movement
  c) loud noise

**10 POT LUCK**

What colour denotes London Underground's Bakerloo line?

ANSWERS ON PAGE 255

# QUIZ 5

**1  MOVIES**
In the *Star Wars* films, which two British actors have played Obi Wan Kenobi?

**2  MUSIC**
What was the Emily Brontë-inspired Number One hit for Kate Bush in 1978?

**3  TV AND RADIO**
Who presented *Desert Island Discs* on Radio 4 for 18 years, from 1987 to 2006?

**4  SPORT AND LEISURE**
In bowls, what is the name of the small white target ball?

**5  HISTORY**
In which year was the Battle of Trafalgar?

**6  GEOGRAPHY**
By area, which is the largest US state?

**7  LITERATURE**
The title of which 1961 Joseph Heller novel has passed into common usage as a phrase meaning a no-win situation?

**8  SCIENCE AND NATURE**
In plants, which green pigment facilitates photosynthesis?

**9  WORDS**
'Trivia' derives from the Latin word for what?
   a) information
   b) tavern
   c) crossroads

**10  POT LUCK**
By what name is the zucchini, a kind of vegetable, better known in the UK?

ANSWERS ON PAGE 255

7

# QUIZ 6

**1 MOVIES**

Who is the monstrous villain in the *Nightmare on Elm Street* movies?

**2 MUSIC**

'Can the Can' and 'Devil Gate Drive' were hits for which 1970s rocker?

**3 TV AND RADIO**

What is Dr Frasier Crane's brother called?

**4 SPORT AND LEISURE**

Which is the most expensive property on the Monopoly® board, Mayfair or Park Lane?

**5 GEOGRAPHY**

What is the capital of Brazil?

**6 SCIENCE AND NATURE**

How many sides does a Möbius strip have?

**7 LITERATURE**

Which literary character rode a horse called Rocinante?

**8 CELEBRITIES**

Thandie Newton starred as Nyah Nordoff-Hall in which Tom Cruise movie from 2000?

**9 WORDS**

What is a 'spurtle'?
- a) a stick for stirring porridge
- b) a very short burst of speed
- c) a surprised movement

**10 POT LUCK**

Who played Julius Caesar in the 1963 movie *Cleopatra* starring Elizabeth Taylor?

ANSWERS ON PAGE 255

# QUIZ 7

**1  MOVIES**
Who is the Oscar-winning father of US actress Angelina Jolie?

**2  MUSIC**
Who wrote the music for the opera *The Magic Flute*?

**3  TV AND RADIO**
Who played Sybil in *Fawlty Towers*?

**4  SPORT AND LEISURE**
Where were the 1948 summer Olympic Games held?

**5  HISTORY**
Which Chinese dynasty ruled from 1368 to 1644?

**6  GEOGRAPHY**
In which country is Strasbourg?

**7  LITERATURE**
In whose novels would you encounter Will Parry and Lyra Belacqua?

**8  SCIENCE AND NATURE**
Which space shuttle exploded on its launch in 1986?

**9  WORDS**
What does 'frangible' mean?
   a) easily broken
   b) tasting of marzipan
   c) moveable through 90 degrees

**10  POT LUCK**
In 1887, a Dr L L Zamenhov created a universal language. What is it called?

ANSWERS ON PAGE 256

# QUIZ 8

**1 MOVIES**
Which actor stars in *Broken Flowers* as a man looking up his old flames, played by Tilda Swinton, Sharon Stone and others?

**2 MUSIC**
'Bicycle Race' and 'Radio Ga Ga' were hits for which group?

**3 TV AND RADIO**
*The Lone Gunmen* was a short-lived spin-off from which 1990s TV series?

**4 SPORT AND LEISURE**
In which ball game is part of the playing area called the apron?

**5 HISTORY**
Simon Bolívar helped drive the Spaniards out of which South American country in 1824?

**6 SCIENCE AND NATURE**
Which Polish-born French physicist died of leukaemia in 1934 following decades of exposure to radiation?

**7 LITERATURE**
Who wrote the series of books for children about St Clare's and Malory Towers schools?

**8 CELEBRITIES**
Julie Christie starred in which landmark 1960s sci-fi BBC TV series?

**9 WORDS**
What is 'edacity'?
        a) lying
        b) laziness
        c) greed

**10 POT LUCK**
Where on the body would you wear epaulettes?

ANSWERS ON PAGE 256

# QUIZ 9

**1 MOVIES**
Which comedy actor and director was born Allen Stewart Konigsberg?

**2 MUSIC**
Madonna's hit 'Beautiful Stranger' featured on the soundtrack of which 1999 film?

**3 TV AND RADIO**
In *The West Wing* Martin Sheen plays POTUS. What does that stand for?

**4 SPORT AND LEISURE**
Which golfer is known as the 'Golden Bear'?

**5 HISTORY**
Who is the Queen's oldest grandchild?

**6 GEOGRAPHY**
What was the former name of the Australian landmark Uluru?

**7 LITERATURE**
Who published *Statecraft* in 2002?

**8 SCIENCE AND NATURE**
Which prehistoric period came between the Cretaceous and the Triassic?

**9 WORDS**
What does an 'ailurophile' like?
   a) gold
   b) the Chinese
   c) cats

**10 POT LUCK**
In Roman mythology, who was the god of fire?

ANSWERS ON PAGE 256

# QUIZ 10

**1  MOVIES**
Janet Leigh and Charlton Heston starred in which classic Orson Welles thriller?

**2  MUSIC**
The characters Papageno and Papagena feature in which Mozart opera?

**3  TV AND RADIO**
Which US sitcom of the 1970s told the surreal story of the Tates and the Campbells?

**4  SPORT AND LEISURE**
Which cricketer captained Middlesex from 1983 to 1997?

**5  HISTORY**
Who was Richard Nixon's first vice president?

**6  SCIENCE AND NATURE**
Phobos and Deimos are satellites of which planet?

**7  LITERATURE**
Who wrote *The Right Stuff* and *Bonfire of the Vanities*?

**8  CELEBRITIES**
In which sci-fi movie did Sharon Stone play Arnold Schwarzenegger's wife?

**9  WORDS**
What is 'zibeline'?
> a) seaweed tendrils
> b) a chocolate dessert
> c) a thick cloth

**10  POT LUCK**
If a creature is 'nucivorous', what does it eat?

ANSWERS ON PAGE 256

# QUIZ 11

**1 MOVIES**
Which Shakespeare play was filmed by the Australian director Baz Luhrmann in 1996 and starred Claire Danes?

**2 MUSIC**
Which duo had a posthumous hit in 1975 with 'The Trail of the Lonesome Pine'?

**3 TV AND RADIO**
David Prowse appeared as which safety-conscious superhero on TV in the 1970s?

**4 SPORT AND LEISURE**
At which sport did Jonah Barrington compete?

**5 HISTORY**
In which century was the Eiffel Tower constructed?

**6 GEOGRAPHY**
Which European capital is built on seven hills, one of which is called the Palatine?

**7 LITERATURE**
Which crime writer disappeared for ten days in 1926?

**8 SCIENCE AND NATURE**
What substance, used in jewellery, is made of fossilized tree resin?

**9 WORDS**
What does 'sinistrorsal' mean?
   a) like the fin of a fish
   b) deeply unsettling
   c) spiralling upwards clockwise

**10 POT LUCK**
Where is Humboldt's Sea?

ANSWERS ON PAGE 256

# QUIZ 12

**1 MOVIES**
Which writer does Nicole Kidman play in *The Hours*?

**2 MUSIC**
Which singer wiggled his backside at Michael Jackson during the 1996 Brit Awards?

**3 TV AND RADIO**
What is the name of Captain Pugwash's ship?

**4 SPORT AND LEISURE**
Which racehorse was kidnapped by the IRA in 1983?

**5 HISTORY**
Which reforming politician became head of state of the USSR in 1988?

**6 SCIENCE AND NATURE**
What is measured on the Réaumur scale?

**7 LITERATURE**
Who wrote the thrillers *The Day of the Jackal* and *The Afghan*?

**8 CELEBRITIES**
Will Ferrell's life is controlled by author Emma Thompson in which 2006 movie?

**9 WORDS**
What is an 'odalisque'?
- a) a standing stone
- b) a concubine
- c) a dance

**10 POT LUCK**
Which motorway runs between Liverpool and Hull?

ANSWERS ON PAGE 256

# QUIZ 13

**1   MOVIES**
Which statue, also the name of the film, was Humphrey Bogart looking for in John Huston's 1941 directorial debut?

**2   MUSIC**
*Danse Macabre* by Saint-Saëns provided the theme music for which TV detective?

**3   TV AND RADIO**
In which TV series did the Wentworth Detention Centre feature?

**4   SPORT AND LEISURE**
Which cricketing hero, who notched up nearly 55,000 runs in his career, had the first names William Gilbert?

**5   HISTORY**
Which 13th-century Italian merchant wrote about his meetings with Kublai Khan?

**6   GEOGRAPHY**
Which man-made waterway bisects Scotland from Inverness in the east to Fort William in the west?

**7   LITERATURE**
Who published *Memoirs of an Unfit Mother* in 2001?

**8   SCIENCE AND NATURE**
What is the next prime number after 13?

**9   WORDS**
What is a 'gnomon'?
  a) a mythical creature
  b) a subatomic particle
  c) part of a sundial

**10   POT LUCK**
From which US writer did Marilyn Monroe get divorced in 1961?

ANSWERS ON PAGE 257

# QUIZ 14

**1  MOVIES**
Gwyneth Paltrow, Brad Pitt and Morgan Freeman starred in which serial killer movie in 1995?

**2  MUSIC**
'Seven Tears' was a 1980s hit for which group?

**3  TV AND RADIO**
To which Mysteron-battling organization does Captain Scarlet belong?

**4  SPORT AND LEISURE**
Who was both the FIFA world player of the year and the European footballer of the year in 2005/2006?

**5  GEOGRAPHY**
Taipei is the capital city of which island country?

**6  SCIENCE AND NATURE**
Where in Pennsylvania was there a nuclear accident in 1979?

**7  LITERATURE**
What is the title of the second volume of *The Lord of the Rings*?

**8  CELEBRITIES**
Jenny Agutter starred as Roberta, and later as Roberta's mother, in film and television adaptations of which novel?

**9  WORDS**
What does 'nugatory' mean?
   a) sweet
   b) of little value
   c) split into pieces

**10  POT LUCK**
Susan, given to the Queen as an 18th birthday present, was Her Majesty's first what?

ANSWERS ON PAGE 257

# QUIZ 15

**1** *MOVIES*
In which city does the bullion robbery take place in 1969's *The Italian Job*?

**2** *MUSIC*
Which band provided a version of Lalo Schifrin's classic theme for *Mission Impossible II*?

**3** *TV AND RADIO*
What kind of animals were Roobarb and Custard?

**4** *SPORT AND LEISURE*
Nick Hornby's 1992 book *Fever Pitch* celebrates which football team?

**5** *HISTORY*
Under which king did England win the Battle of Agincourt?

**6** *GEOGRAPHY*
What is the capital city of Cuba?

**7** *LITERATURE*
What is the name of Sherlock Holmes's brother?

**8** *SCIENCE AND NATURE*
With which invention is John Logie Baird associated?

**9** *WORDS*
What is an 'autodidact'?
        a) a self-taught person
        b) an unelected ruler
        c) a single-seater aircraft

**10** *POT LUCK*
Which is the fifth book of the Old Testament?

ANSWERS ON PAGE 257

# QUIZ 16

**1  MOVIES**

In which movie did Burt Reynolds play an adult movie director called Jack Horner?

**2  MUSIC**

John Philip Sousa's *Liberty Bell March* was used as the theme music of which TV programme?

**3  TV AND RADIO**

Who is Patty and Selma Bouvier's more famous sister?

**4  SPORT AND LEISURE**

Which sport was originally named 'mintonette' after its resemblance to badminton?

**5  GEOGRAPHY**

Which US state has the nicknames 'the Mormon state' and 'the Beehive state'?

**6  SCIENCE AND NATURE**

In which country is the Semmering Railway, a World Heritage site?

**7  LITERATURE**

Siegfried and Tristan Farnon appear in a series of books by which author?

**8  CELEBRITIES**

Juliette Binoche and Kristin Scott Thomas starred with Ralph Fiennes in which 1990s Oscar-winning movie?

**9  WORDS**

'Mirepoix' is a mixture of what?
- a) germs
- b) paint
- c) vegetables

**10  POT LUCK**

Old Scratch and Old Nick are both nicknames for whom?

ANSWERS ON PAGE 257

# QUIZ 17

**1 MOVIES**
Who provides the voice of Rocky in Nick Park's animated movie *Chicken Run*?

**2 MUSIC**
Which group released an album called *Blue Lines* in 1991?

**3 TV AND RADIO**
Joanne Whalley, star of the movies *Scandal* and *Willow*, had an early acting break in which Dennis Potter TV drama?

**4 SPORT AND LEISURE**
Who won the women's singles final at Wimbledon in the Queen's Silver Jubilee year?

**5 HISTORY**
What was the John F Kennedy International Airport in New York formerly commonly known as?

**6 GEOGRAPHY**
On which Pacific island, also known as Rapa Nui, would you find giant carved stone heads?

**7 LITERATURE**
The world succumbs to deadly walking plants in which classic 1950s novel by John Wyndham?

**8 SCIENCE AND NATURE**
What is the first element in the periodic table?

**9 WORDS**
What does 'sesquipedalian' mean?
        a) 150 years old
        b) prone to using long words
        c) powered by pedals

**10 POT LUCK**
In the human body, which muscle is attached at only one end?

ANSWERS ON PAGE 257

# QUIZ 18

**1 MOVIES**
Mia Farrow played the mother of a possessed child in which 1960s Roman Polanski film?

**2 MUSIC**
Which 1970s singer's first hit was 'My Coo-Ca-Choo'?

**3 TV AND RADIO**
Which TV presenter links *Newsround*, *Multi-Coloured Swap Shop* and *Country File*?

**4 SPORT AND LEISURE**
What is a 'widow' in some card games?

**5 HISTORY**
Which US civil rights leader was assassinated by James Earl Ray in 1968?

**6 SCIENCE AND NATURE**
What colour are amethysts?

**7 LITERATURE**
Who married Anne Hathaway in 1582?

**8 CELEBRITIES**
In which Tom Cruise movie, directed by Steven Spielberg, did Samantha Morton appear?

**9 WORDS**
If something is 'tenebrous', is it ... ?
        a) dark
        b) loud
        c) unlikely

**10 POT LUCK**
Which wedding anniversary is associated with wood?

ANSWERS ON PAGE 257

# QUIZ 19

**1  MOVIES**
In the 1980s, who rode in a specially converted ambulance bearing the registration number ECTO-1?

**2  MUSIC**
Who sang with the 1990 England World Cup squad on the single 'World in Motion'?

**3  TV AND RADIO**
Which actor connects *Basil Brush*, *Yes Minister* and *Heartbeat*?

**4  SPORT AND LEISURE**
Who won the first Rugby Union World Cup in 1987?

**5  HISTORY**
Which Carthaginian soldier marched his army, with elephants, across the Alps in an attack on Rome in 218 BC?

**6  GEOGRAPHY**
Of which country is Vilnius the capital?

**7  LITERATURE**
Who wrote the three novels that make up *The Forsyte Saga*?

**8  SCIENCE AND NATURE**
Which animal, native to Mauritius, was hunted to extinction in the 17th century?

**9  WORDS**
What is 'moxibustion'?
  a) a skin treatment
  b) a fuel refining process
  c) a state of extreme weariness

**10  POT LUCK**
It was originally a cup with a rounded base which wouldn't stand up, meaning the contents had to be drunk in one go. We still use the word today to describe a glass. What is it?

ANSWERS ON PAGE 258

# QUIZ 20

**1  MOVIES**
In which movie did Groucho Marx play Rufus T Firefly, the dictator of Freedonia?

**2  MUSIC**
Who composed the classical pieces *Water Music* and *Music for the Royal Fireworks*?

**3  TV AND RADIO**
Robert Wagner and Stefanie Powers played husband-and-wife sleuths in which 1970s and 1980s TV show?

**4  SPORT AND LEISURE**
Who is the only boxer ever to have knocked out George Foreman?

**5  GEOGRAPHY**
The island of Hispaniola contains the Dominican Republic and which other country?

**6  SCIENCE AND NATURE**
The cephalic index is a measurement of which part of the human body?

**7  LITERATURE**
Which sinister fictional criminal was created by Sax Rohmer?

**8  CELEBRITIES**
Helen Mirren played Bob Hoskins's wife in which British gangster film?

**9  WORDS**
In the USSR, what was 'samizdat'?
        a) black tea
        b) dissident literature
        c) public transport

**10  POT LUCK**
Which character did Roger Lloyd Pack play in *Only Fools and Horses*?

ANSWERS ON PAGE 258

# QUIZ 21

**1 MOVIES**

Which lead actor, more famous for his comedy roles, played the grumpy Transit Authority Inspector hero in 1974's *The Taking of Pelham One Two Three*?

**2 MUSIC**

Whose albums include *Are You Experienced* and *Electric Ladyland*?

**3 TV AND RADIO**

Which veteran Radio 1 DJ was also the host of Radio 4's *Home Truths*?

**4 SPORT AND LEISURE**

Which Stoke City and England goalkeeper's career effectively ended when he injured his eye in a road accident in 1972?

**5 HISTORY**

What headgear takes its name from an 1854 battle?

**6 GEOGRAPHY**

St Peter Port is the capital of which island?

**7 LITERATURE**

Which former British prime minister won the Nobel Prize for literature in 1953?

**8 SCIENCE AND NATURE**

Which British scientist formulated the three laws of motion, published in a work known as the *Principia*?

**9 WORDS**

'Bumf', meaning paperwork, is short for which crude old-fashioned term for toilet paper?

**10 POT LUCK**

The actor Michael Douglas first came to prominence in which US TV cop show?

ANSWERS ON PAGE 258

# QUIZ 22

**1  MOVIES**
For which film did Diane Keaton win the Best Actress Oscar in 1977?

**2  MUSIC**
'Goldfinger', 'Oh Yeah' and 'A Life Less Ordinary' were 1990s hits for which band?

**3  TV AND RADIO**
In which 1970s Japanese TV drama did 108 warriors fight corruption in Lian Shan Po?

**4  SPORT AND LEISURE**
In which year did Venus Williams first become the Wimbledon women's singles champion?

**5  HISTORY**
From which ship did Nelson direct the fleet at Trafalgar?

**6  SCIENCE AND NATURE**
Which bone-softening children's disease, often resulting in bow legs, is caused by insufficient vitamin D?

**7  LITERATURE**
Which Russian dramatist wrote *The Cherry Orchard* and *Uncle Vanya*?

**8  CELEBRITIES**
Ellen DeGeneres played the voice of Dory in which animated film?

**9  WORDS**
What is a planet's 'albedo'?
> a) the proportion of light it reflects
> b) the amount of ice in its poles
> c) its gravitational attraction

**10  POT LUCK**
In golf, how many strokes under par is an albatross?

ANSWERS ON PAGE 258

# QUIZ 23

**1  MOVIES**

Pelé, Michael Caine and Sylvester Stallone once starred in a film together. What was it called?

**2  MUSIC**

Which group of comedians sang with Cliff Richard on the 1986 reworking of his hit 'Living Doll'?

**3  TV AND RADIO**

Which Welsh steam engine, looked after by Jones the Steam, gave his name to the animated series in which he starred?

**4  SPORT AND LEISURE**

Which famous US horse race has been run over 1 mile and 2 furlongs in Churchill Downs, Louisville, since 1875?

**5  HISTORY**

In which country did the Boxer Rising of 1900 take place?

**6  GEOGRAPHY**

What name was given to the towns of Sandwich, Dover, Hythe, Romney and Hastings?

**7  LITERATURE**

Which Dublin-born writer did both Kate Winslet and Dame Judi Dench portray on film in 2001?

**8  SCIENCE AND NATURE**

Between which two planets would you find the asteroid belt?

**9  WORDS**

What does 'recherché' mean?
- a) hard to do
- b) carefully chosen
- c) covered with feathers

**10  POT LUCK**

After which US president, known for his love of hunting, is the Teddy Bear named?

ANSWERS ON PAGE 258

# QUIZ 24

**1  MOVIES**
In which movie did Charlize Theron portray the USA's first convicted female serial killer?

**2  MUSIC**
With whom did Kenny Rogers duet on his hit 'Islands in the Stream'?

**3  TV AND RADIO**
Which *Doctor Who* villains come from the planet Skaro?

**4  SPORT AND LEISURE**
In bingo, what number was denoted by the call 'kelly's eye'?

**5  GEOGRAPHY**
Of which country is Kathmandu the capital?

**6  SCIENCE AND NATURE**
When white wines are 'maderized', they have become tinged through old age with what colour?

**7  LITERATURE**
Jacqueline Susann also wrote *The Love Machine*, but for which novel is she mainly remembered?

**8  CELEBRITIES**
Which Scottish actor played the brother of Rachel Weisz in *The Mummy* and *The Mummy Returns*?

**9  WORDS**
What would you use a 'quern' for?
> a) restraining a horse
> b) grinding corn
> c) holding arrows

**10  POT LUCK**
What was the name of the animated cat created in 1919 by Otto Messmer?

ANSWERS ON PAGE 258

# QUIZ 25

**1  MOVIES**
John Cleese's character in *A Fish Called Wanda* is called
Archibald Leach. To which actor, whose real name was Archibald
Leach, is this a tribute?

**2  MUSIC**
Which US singer changed his name from Robert Zimmerman?

**3  TV AND RADIO**
A mainstay of *Coronation Street* in the 1960s and 1970s, what
was the name of the work-shy window cleaner played by Bernard
Youens?

**4  SPORT AND LEISURE**
Which Formula One driver died in a crash in the 1994 San Marino
Grand Prix?

**5  HISTORY**
The death of which English king is shown in the Bayeux tapestry?

**6  GEOGRAPHY**
Which group of islands, a self-governing region of Denmark, can
be found between Iceland and the Shetland Islands?

**7  LITERATURE**
Who wrote *Paradise Lost*?

**8  SCIENCE AND NATURE**
To what animal does the word 'struthious' relate?

**9  WORDS**
What is a 'plenipotentiary'?
>        a) an ornate lavatory
>        b) a large amount of money
>        c) an authorized diplomat

**10  POT LUCK**
The HMV logo depicts a dog staring into an old gramophone
horn. For what do the initials HMV stand?

ANSWERS ON PAGE 259

# QUIZ 26

1 **MOVIES**
In which 1990s movie thriller does Sean Penn play Michael Douglas's brother?

2 **MUSIC**
'When Doves Cry', 'Purple Rain' and 'Batdance' were all hits for which singer?

3 **TV AND RADIO**
Which TV naturalist's work includes the series *Life on Earth*, *The Living Planet* and *Life in the Freezer*?

4 **SPORT AND LEISURE**
How is the basketball team that turned professional in 1927 under the name Savoy Big Five better known these days?

5 **HISTORY**
Journalists Bob Woodward and Carl Bernstein were instrumental in exposing which 1970s political scandal?

6 **SCIENCE AND NATURE**
Which Russian behaviourist is remembered largely for his conditioning experiments involving salivating dogs?

7 **LITERATURE**
Who wrote the racing thrillers *Wild Horses* and *Come to Grief*?

8 **CELEBRITIES**
In which 1970s movie did Warren Beatty star with Julie Christie, Goldie Hawn and a young Carrie Fisher?

9 **WORDS**
Where would you find a 'proscenium arch'?
        a) a theatre
        b) a church
        c) a barrister's chambers

10 **POT LUCK**
What is the surname of the French brothers credited with the world's first manned balloon flight?

ANSWERS ON PAGE 259

# QUIZ 27

**1 MOVIES**

In which movie would you find the characters Caractacus Potts, Truly Scrumptious and the Child Catcher?

**2 MUSIC**

Which 1962 Little Eva hit did Kylie Minogue cover in 1988?

**3 TV AND RADIO**

What is the name of the TV series starring Kiefer Sutherland whose story spans one action-packed day and which is broadcast as though in real time?

**4 SPORT AND LEISURE**

Before changing his name on joining the Black Muslims in 1964, what was Muhammad Ali called?

**5 HISTORY**

In which year did the Berlin Wall come down?

**6 GEOGRAPHY**

A mountain of volcanic origin called Arthur's Seat can be found in which European city?

**7 LITERATURE**

What do the initials 'J K' stand for in the name of the *Harry Potter* author J K Rowling?

**8 SCIENCE AND NATURE**

How many faces does a dodecahedron have?

**9 WORDS**

What is 'alliteration' the use of?
- a) words which rhyme
- b) words which begin with the same sound
- c) words with the same number of syllables

**10 POT LUCK**

Which British actress changed her name from Diana Fluck?

ANSWERS ON PAGE 259

# QUIZ 28

**1  MOVIES**

Anne Hathaway and Meryl Streep both appeared in 2006 in which movie set in the fashion industry?

**2  MUSIC**

'Uptown Girl', 'Tell Her About It' and 'River of Dreams' were all hits for which singer and pianist?

**3  TV AND RADIO**

In which TV series were the two main characters called Danny Wilde and Lord Brett Sinclair?

**4  SPORT AND LEISURE**

Which board game's name means 'I play' in Latin?

**5  HISTORY**

Which document did King John sign at Runnymede in 1215?

**6  SCIENCE AND NATURE**

What is the name of the visual telegraphy system in which two hand-held flags are used?

**7  ART**

Which French impressionist painted *Water Lilies* and *Rouen Cathedral* among other works?

**8  CELEBRITIES**

*Lethal Weapon* 2 star Patsy Kensit went on to appear in which UK TV soap opera?

**9  WORDS**

What is 'marl'?
> a) a fruit compote
> b) a sedimentary clay
> c) an animal dropping

**10  POT LUCK**

In which TV comedy sketch show do Daffyd, Bubbles and Lou and Andy regularly appear?

ANSWERS ON PAGE 259

# QUIZ 29

**1   MOVIES**
Kirsten Dunst, star of *Spider-Man*, made an early appearance as an immortal 12-year-old in which 1994 Tom Cruise movie?

**2   MUSIC**
Which German composer wrote *Fingal's Cave*?

**3   TV AND RADIO**
Which acerbic Yorkshireman has fronted both *Newsnight* and *University Challenge* on BBC2?

**4   SPORT AND LEISURE**
Which English footballer called his autobiography *Psycho* after his team nickname?

**5   HISTORY**
The phrase 'Once and Future King' was coined by Sir Thomas Malory in his account of which regal figure?

**6   GEOGRAPHY**
Addis Ababa is the capital of which country?

**7   LITERATURE**
Which British writer was born Eric Arthur Blair?

**8   SCIENCE AND NATURE**
In what SI unit is electrical current measured?

**9   WORDS**
What is a 'penumbra'?
        a) a half-shadow
        b) a character in calligraphy
        c) a cantilevered item of underwear

**10   POT LUCK**
Whose face reputedly 'launch'd a thousand ships'?

ANSWERS ON PAGE 259

# QUIZ 30

**1 MOVIES**
Maureen O'Hara starred with John Wayne in which whimsical John Ford comedy set in Galway?

**2 MUSIC**
Which 1980s singer changed his name from Stuart Goddard?

**3 TV AND RADIO**
What is the name of the boozing, smoking and gambling robot in *Futurama*?

**4 SPORT AND LEISURE**
In which leisure activity might you purl, cast on or cast off?

**5 HISTORY**
How many elected Members of Parliament make up the House of Commons?

**6 SCIENCE AND NATURE**
By what name is the 'scapula' more commonly known?

**7 LITERATURE**
Which contemporary bestselling author has written books called *The Fifth Elephant*, *Soul Music* and *The Colour of Magic*?

**8 CELEBRITIES**
Parker Posey appeared in which Christopher Guest comedy movie set around a competitive dog show?

**9 WORDS**
What is a 'goglet'?
- a) an optical instrument
- b) a diving bird
- c) a water cooler

**10 POT LUCK**
Which instrument derives its name from the Hawaiian phrase for 'jumping flea'?

ANSWERS ON PAGE 259

# QUIZ 31

**1 MOVIES**

Which 1994 movie centred upon a bus that was wired to explode if it dropped below 50mph?

**2 MUSIC**

With which group, whose hits included 'Dirty Old Town' and 'Fiesta', was Shane MacGowan the lead singer?

**3 TV AND RADIO**

Which comedian appeared alongside 'Monkey' in television adverts for the ill-fated ITV Digital channel?

**4 SPORT AND LEISURE**

Uncompromising footballers Billy Bremner, Norman Hunter and Vinnie Jones have all played for which English football team?

**5 HISTORY**

Which legendary character was the original Peeping Tom supposed to have spied on?

**6 GEOGRAPHY**

On which island group would you find Skara Brae, Maes Howe and the Churchill Barriers?

**7 LITERATURE**

Holden Caulfield is the central character in which novel?

**8 SCIENCE AND NATURE**

Where in the body would you find bones called hammer, anvil and stirrup?

**9 WORDS**

What is an 'acinus'?
- a) a toe infection
- b) the highest note of a piece of music
- c) an individual section of a fruit like a raspberry

**10 POT LUCK**

Where is Sidney Sussex college?

ANSWERS ON PAGE 260

# QUIZ 32

**1 MOVIES**
Which screen legend's final appearance was in the 1956 movie *The Harder They Fall*?

**2 MUSIC**
Which musician famously called his daughter Moon Unit?

**3 TV AND RADIO**
Which long-running TV quiz has a theme tune called 'Approaching Menace'?

**4 SPORT AND LEISURE**
Who managed the England football team from 1974 to 1977?

**5 GEOGRAPHY**
In Mexico, 100 centavos make what unit of currency?

**6 SCIENCE AND NATURE**
What order of mammal are opossums, bandicoots, koalas and wombats?

**7 LITERATURE**
Who wrote *Captain Corelli's Mandolin*?

**8 CELEBRITIES**
What kind of broadcaster does Nicole Kidman play in *To Die For*?

**9 WORDS**
What is 'osculation'?
    a) kissing
    b) slapping
    c) apologizing

**10 POT LUCK**
Which divinity in the Hindu pantheon is known as the destroyer?

ANSWERS ON PAGE 260

34

# QUIZ 33

**1  MOVIES**

Humphrey Bogart and Katharine Hepburn sailed which boat through East Africa in 1951?

**2  MUSIC**

Geri Halliwell contributed which song to the *Bridget Jones's Diary* soundtrack?

**3  TV AND RADIO**

Frank Furillo, Joyce Davenport, Phil Esterhaus and Howard Hunter were characters in which groundbreaking police TV drama series of the 1980s?

**4  SPORT AND LEISURE**

Which snooker player was nicknamed the 'Whirlwind'?

**5  HISTORY**

Who was king of England during the American War of Independence?

**6  GEOGRAPHY**

In which ocean are the Seychelles?

**7  LITERATURE**

Who wrote the *Famous Five* and *Secret Seven* children's books?

**8  SCIENCE AND NATURE**

Which prehistoric fish was thought to be long extinct until a living specimen was caught in 1938?

**9  WORDS**

What is an 'abecedarian'?
a) an ancient Scot
b) a black magician
c) someone learning the alphabet

**10  POT LUCK**

Who is fourth in line to the British throne?

ANSWERS ON PAGE 260

# QUIZ 34

**1  MOVIES**
In which movie does Tom Hanks fall in love with a mermaid played by Daryl Hannah?

**2  MUSIC**
How many strings are there usually on a mandolin?

**3  TV AND RADIO**
Esther Rantzen, Cyril Fletcher and Paul Heiney were all regulars on which long-running BBC consumer affairs programme?

**4  SPORT AND LEISURE**
In which sport does Beth Tweddle excel?

**5  GEOGRAPHY**
Of which Canadian province is Winnipeg the capital?

**6  SCIENCE AND NATURE**
Other than tin, what is the main constituent of pewter?

**7  LITERATURE**
Pinkie is the main character in which Graham Greene novel?

**8  CELEBRITIES**
Brigitte Nielsen plays a sword-wielding barbarian in which Arnold Schwarzenegger movie of the 1980s?

**9  WORDS**
What is a Maori 'wahine'?
        a) a tattoo
        b) a woman
        c) a home

**10  POT LUCK**
An epidemic of which disease caused the cancellation of the Cheltenham Gold Cup in 2001?

ANSWERS ON PAGE 260

# QUIZ 35

**1  MOVIES**

With which film did Gus Van Sant win the Palme d'Or at the Cannes film festival in 2003?

**2  MUSIC**

Which hard rocking British band had a hit with 'The Ace Of Spades' in 1980 and again in 1993?

**3  TV AND RADIO**

In which revered kids' programme would you have found Geoffrey, George, Bungle and Zippy?

**4  SPORT AND LEISURE**

Who scored England's fifth goal in their 5–1 defeat of Germany in September 2001?

**5  HISTORY**

Which British prime minister claimed to have secured 'peace in our time' before the outbreak of World War II?

**6  GEOGRAPHY**

Near which French city does the Channel Tunnel emerge?

**7  LITERATURE**

Under which pseudonym did Mary Ann Evans write?

**8  SCIENCE AND NATURE**

At two o'clock, how many degrees separate the hands on a conventional clock face, reading clockwise from the minute hand?

**9  WORDS**

What is 'phrenology'?
- a) reading palms
- b) reading auras
- c) reading bumps on the head

**10  POT LUCK**

What was the name of Gillian Anderson's character in *The X Files*?

ANSWERS ON PAGE 260

# QUIZ 36

**1  MOVIES**

Which Mexican actor, who later starred in *Babel*, played Che Guevara in the 2004 film *The Motorcycle Diaries*?

**2  MUSIC**

Diana Ross had a Top Ten hit in 1981 singing 'Endless Love' with which male singer?

**3  TV AND RADIO**

Harry Enfield, John Sessions, Rory Bremner and Steve Coogan all provided voices for which satirical TV puppet show?

**4  SPORT AND LEISURE**

Which sport has a 122cm diameter target, with ten rings ranging from the ten-point gold inner to the one-point white outer?

**5  HISTORY**

What is the name given to the theft of more than £25 million worth of gold bullion from Heathrow on 26 November 1983?

**6  SCIENCE AND NATURE**

King, emperor and fairy are all types of which creature?

**7  LITERATURE**

Grenouille is the unpleasant central character of which Patrick Suskind novel?

**8  CELEBRITIES**

Which British comedian starred as an Indian doctor alongside Sophia Loren in *The Millionairess*?

**9  WORDS**

What is a 'rebec'?
- a) a medieval instrument
- b) a Canadian moose
- c) a Turkish garment

**10  POT LUCK**

Who was the father of Icarus?

ANSWERS ON PAGE 260

# QUIZ 37

**1   MOVIES**

Which US actor has played an institutionalized convict in *The Shawshank Redemption*, a world-weary cop in *Se7en* and the US president in *Deep Impact*?

**2   MUSIC**

Whose real name was McKinley Morganfield?

**3   TV AND RADIO**

Which former Radio 1 DJ was known as the 'Hairy Cornflake'?

**4   SPORT AND LEISURE**

Austrian Franz Klammer was a 1976 Olympic gold medallist in which event?

**5   HISTORY**

What was the middle name of disgraced US president Richard Nixon?

**6   GEOGRAPHY**

What is the largest city in Alaska?

**7   LITERATURE**

Who wrote the classic *Just So* stories and the ever-popular poem *If*?

**8   SCIENCE AND NATURE**

Which two elements make up water?

**9   WORDS**

From where does the 'éclair' get its name?
- a) the French word for cream
- b) the French word for lightning
- c) the French word for cylinder

**10   POT LUCK**

What is the name of the brandy distilled from the fermented remains of crushed grapes?

ANSWERS ON PAGE 261

# QUIZ 38

**1 MOVIES**
Greta Garbo, Fredric March and Basil Rathbone starred in which 1930s movie adaptation of a Tolstoy novel?

**2 MUSIC**
Which Spanish city provided the title for Freddie Mercury and Montserrat Caballé's Top Ten hit?

**3 TV AND RADIO**
Lulu and Julie Walters both played the TV mother of which troubled adolescent boy?

**4 SPORT AND LEISURE**
Which Irish golfer completed an accountancy degree before turning professional?

**5 HISTORY**
Which Indian leader was assassinated in 1948?

**6 SCIENCE AND NATURE**
By which of the body's organs is insulin secreted?

**7 LITERATURE**
Which crime writer, who died in 2006, was responsible for the Mike Hammer novels?

**8 CELEBRITIES**
In which scary movie does Robin Williams unnervingly play Sy the Photo Guy?

**9 WORDS**
In music, 'rallentando' means becoming gradually what?
- a) louder
- b) higher
- c) slower

**10 POT LUCK**
Which British military rank comes between colonel and major-general?

ANSWERS ON PAGE 261

# QUIZ 39

**1   MOVIES**
Penelope Cruz starred with Nicolas Cage in which 2001 adaptation of a literary bestseller?

**2   MUSIC**
Which composer's life was the basis for the movie *Amadeus*?

**3   TV AND RADIO**
What is the name of the snail in *The Magic Roundabout*?

**4   SPORT AND LEISURE**
A diminutive Russian gymnast won three gold medals and one silver medal at the 1972 Olympics. What was her name?

**5   HISTORY**
When Rome was devastated by fire in AD 64, which emperor, who supposedly enjoyed the spectacle, was in power?

**6   GEOGRAPHY**
Which major geographical feature did Michael Palin visit for a 2002 TV series, visiting ten countries, one disputed territory and travelling 10,000 miles?

**7   LITERATURE**
Who wrote *Flowers in the Attic* and still manages to produce a new book each year despite her death in 1986?

**8   SCIENCE AND NATURE**
Which chemical element has the symbol Sn?

**9   WORDS**
What is 'dactylography'?
- a) the study of fingerprints
- b) the study of dinosaurs
- c) the study of handwriting

**10   POT LUCK**
What is the name of the leather trousers traditionally worn by men in Austria and Bavaria?

ANSWERS ON PAGE 261

# QUIZ 40

**1 MOVIES**
Madeleine Stowe and Daniel Day-Lewis starred in which Michael Mann movie of a James Fenimore Cooper book?

**2 MUSIC**
Who sang with Bing Crosby on his hit song 'Road to Morocco'?

**3 TV AND RADIO**
Who played Jim Rockford in *The Rockford Files*?

**4 SPORT AND LEISURE**
'Whiff whaff' and 'flim flam' were early alternative names for which indoor game?

**5 GEOGRAPHY**
Antananarivo is the capital of which African island nation?

**6 SCIENCE AND NATURE**
In computing, what does DOS stand for?

**7 LITERATURE**
Samuel Langhorne Clemens was the real name of which US author?

**8 CELEBRITIES**
Which Radio 2 DJ's listeners are known as TOGs?

**9 WORDS**
With what substance does a 'currier' work?
  a) glass
  b) paper
  c) leather

**10 POT LUCK**
Which country is identified by the internet suffix .de?

ANSWERS ON PAGE 261

42

# QUIZ 41

**1 MOVIES**

In which 1992 Wesley Snipes film did Liz Hurley play an air hostess?

**2 MUSIC**

Which group recorded the influential album *Pet Sounds* in 1966?

**3 TV AND RADIO**

Who played both Father Dougal in *Father Ted* and Thermoman in *My Hero*?

**4 SPORT AND LEISURE**

In what sport do teams vie for the Stanley Cup?

**5 HISTORY**

Who killed Abraham Lincoln?

**6 GEOGRAPHY**

Which English city did the Romans know as Aquae Sulis?

**7 LITERATURE**

Who wrote the *Just William* stories?

**8 SCIENCE AND NATURE**

Which part of the body gets its name from a shortened form of a Latin phrase meaning 'twelve fingers' length'?

**9 WORDS**

What does 'pleonasm' mean?
- a) a component part of blood
- b) an unnecessary word
- c) a transparent plastic

**10 POT LUCK**

Which drink gets its name from the Gaelic words *uisge beatha*, literally meaning 'water of life'?

ANSWERS ON PAGE 261

# QUIZ 42

**1 MOVIES**

Maggie Gyllenhaal played James Spader's submissive personal assistant in which challenging movie comedy?

**2 MUSIC**

Who composed the *Pink Panther* theme?

**3 TV AND RADIO**

In which TV series did the Cartwright family manage the Ponderosa ranch?

**4 SPORT AND LEISURE**

Which boxer, who died in 1989, was originally named Walker Smith?

**5 HISTORY**

In 1997, what was returned by the UK to China?

**6 SCIENCE AND NATURE**

Which US test pilot was the first person to break the sound barrier?

**7 LITERATURE**

Which Mario Puzo novel was filmed to great effect by Francis Ford Coppola in 1972?

**8 CELEBRITIES**

Lesley-Anne Down plays Jacqueline Payne Marone in which US TV soap opera?

**9 WORDS**

What is a 'cheongsam'?
  a) a Chinese dress
  b) a throwing weapon
  c) a wooden puzzle

**10 POT LUCK**

By which deadly nickname was hospital cook Mary Mallon better known in the early 20th century?

ANSWERS ON PAGE 261

# QUIZ 43

**1  MOVIES**
*Charlie's Angels* star Drew Barrymore made a very early appearance in which 1982 Steven Spielberg movie?

**2  MUSIC**
Which band's singles in the 1960s and 1970s included 'The Weight', 'Up on Cripple Creek' and 'Rag Mama Rag'?

**3  TV AND RADIO**
Which genial Irish comedian was the original host of *Catchphrase*?

**4  SPORT AND LEISURE**
Under whose captaincy did the English cricket team regain the Ashes from Australia in the Test series of 1953?

**5  HISTORY**
Which Caribbean island gained its independence from Britain in 1962, led by Sir Alexander Bustamante?

**6  GEOGRAPHY**
In which city would you find Sugar Loaf Mountain?

**7  LITERATURE**
Under what name did Frederick Dannay and Manfred B Lee publish detective novels?

**8  SCIENCE AND NATURE**
What is the largest body in the solar system?

**9  WORDS**
What is a 'prestidigitator'?
  a) a conjuror
  b) a computer operator
  c) a large reptile

**10  POT LUCK**
*Entrechat* and *pas de deux* are terms used in which field?

ANSWERS ON PAGE 262

# QUIZ 44

**1 MOVIES**

In which heist movie does Julia Roberts play a fictional character forced into impersonating the real Julia Roberts?

**2 MUSIC**

Which veteran rock band began a long-running world tour entitled 'A Bigger Bang' in 2005?

**3 TV AND RADIO**

Purdey, Gambit and Steed were the three central characters in which TV series?

**4 SPORT AND LEISURE**

'Whispering' Ted Lowe was famous for commentating on which sport?

**5 GEOGRAPHY**

Minsk is the capital city of which East European republic?

**6 SCIENCE AND NATURE**

Which UK pioneer is credited with inventing the jet engine?

**7 LITERATURE**

Which poet did Elizabeth Barrett marry in 1846?

**8 CELEBRITIES**

In which Spike Lee movie did Jodie Foster, Denzel Washington and Clive Owen star?

**9 WORDS**

If you 'dulcify' something, do you make it ...?
- a) boring
- b) sweet
- c) bony

**10 POT LUCK**

Which bridge in Venice connects the Doge's Palace with Pozzi Prison?

ANSWERS ON PAGE 262

# QUIZ 45

**1  MOVIES**
*The Gold Rush* and *The Great Dictator* were the work of which English actor and director?

**2  MUSIC**
For which album did Paul Simon win a Grammy Award in 1987?

**3  TV AND RADIO**
In which British TV show, which ran from 1955 to 1976, did Jack Warner coin the phrase 'Evening All'?

**4  SPORT AND LEISURE**
Although more famous for his subsequent acting career, he originally shot to fame as the first person to swim 100m in less than a minute. Who was he?

**5  HISTORY**
Who was Henry VIII's sixth wife?

**6  GEOGRAPHY**
What is the name of the long narrow inlets between steep cliffs that are abundant in Norway?

**7  LITERATURE**
Who writes the *Sharpe* novels?

**8  SCIENCE AND NATURE**
'Cumulonimbus' and 'cumulostratus' are types of what?

**9  WORDS**
What does 'puerile' mean?
  a) like an ass
  b) like an idiot
  c) like a child

**10  POT LUCK**
Which British city has the telephone area code 0141?

ANSWERS ON PAGE 262

# QUIZ 46

**1 MOVIES**
Which 1980s epic flop starred Sting and Francesca Annis among others, and had a soundtrack by the band Toto?

**2 MUSIC**
*Danse Macabre* and *Carnaval des Animaux* were the work of which French composer?

**3 TV AND RADIO**
Which actor played Carter in the 1990s sitcom *Nightingales*?

**4 SPORT AND LEISURE**
Who was the fourth oarsman with Foster, Pinsent and Redgrave in the successful British coxless four at the Sydney Olympics?

**5 GEOGRAPHY**
In which continent is the Limpopo river?

**6 SCIENCE AND NATURE**
Which scientist formulated the special and general theories of relativity?

**7 LITERATURE**
*Mourning Becomes Elektra* and *The Iceman Cometh* are plays by which US dramatist?

**8 CELEBRITIES**
Perry, Schwimmer and LeBlanc were the surnames of the three male principal actors in which US TV series?

**9 WORDS**
Which animals are described as 'limacine'?
> a) slugs
> b) horses
> c) kestrels

**10 POT LUCK**
Which poker hand consists of three of a kind and a pair?

ANSWERS ON PAGE 262

# QUIZ 47

**1 MOVIES**

Which Hollywood star had leading roles in *LA Confidential*, *The Time Machine*, *Memento* and the long-running TV soap *Neighbours*?

**2 MUSIC**

The D'Oyly Carte opera company is famed for performing whose works?

**3 TV AND RADIO**

Which soap opera was set in the Australian town of Summer Bay?

**4 SPORT AND LEISURE**

Which legendary Scottish football manager took Celtic to nine championships in a row and later took Scotland to the World Cup finals in Spain in 1982?

**5 HISTORY**

Which soldier and politician staged a coup in Uganda in 1971?

**6 GEOGRAPHY**

Which man-made feature links the Mediterranean with the Red Sea?

**7 LITERATURE**

Who was working on a novel called *Sanditon* when she died?

**8 SCIENCE AND NATURE**

Which planet has satellites called Phobos and Deimos?

**9 WORDS**

What does 'nacreous' mean?
- a) crumbly
- b) deadly
- c) pearly

**10 POT LUCK**

Which programme originally took us through the arched window, the round window or the square window?

ANSWERS ON PAGE 262

# QUIZ 48

**1   MOVIES**
In which 1980 comedy film does Goldie Hawn join the army?

**2   MUSIC**
'Cool for Cats', 'Up the Junction' and 'Labelled with Love' were all hit singles for which group?

**3   TV AND RADIO**
Big Bird, Oscar the Grouch and Cookie Monster were characters in which educational programme?

**4   SPORT AND LEISURE**
Which black US athlete upset Hitler by winning four gold medals at the 1936 Berlin Olympics?

**5   HISTORY**
Who, as special envoy of the Archbishop of Canterbury, was kidnapped in Beirut in 1987 and not released until 1991?

**6   SCIENCE AND NATURE**
Which organ of the body is affected by the disease 'trachoma'?

**7   LITERATURE**
Which London writer's published diary runs from 1 January 1660 to 31 May 1669?

**8   CELEBRITIES**
Gwyneth Paltrow starred with Matt Damon in which movie adaptation of a Patricia Highsmith novel?

**9   WORDS**
What is a 'shrike'?
>        a) a medieval weapon
>        b) a cut-off scream
>        c) a bird

**10   POT LUCK**
'Gimel' is the third letter of which alphabet?

ANSWERS ON PAGE 262

# QUIZ 49

**1 MOVIES**

In which classic movie does Audrey Hepburn sing 'Moon River'?

**2 MUSIC**

Bryan Adams's record '(Everything I Do) I Do It For You' reached Number One in the UK in July 1991. Which Irish group finally knocked it off the top spot in November that year?

**3 TV AND RADIO**

What was the name of Granada's soap opera, set in a covered market in Manchester, which ran only from 1985 to 1986?

**4 SPORT AND LEISURE**

In which sport would you find the Green Bay Packers, the Miami Dolphins and the Pittsburgh Steelers?

**5 HISTORY**

Which Labour politician, who was born in Bradford in 1910 and who died in 2002, was responsible for the introduction of the breathalyser and the 70mph speed limit?

**6 GEOGRAPHY**

In the USA what are Yellowstone, Yosemite and the Petrified Forest examples of?

**7 LITERATURE**

*Catcher in the Rye* is the most famous work of which reclusive author?

**8 SCIENCE AND NATURE**

In the expression $E=mc^2$, what constant does 'c' represent?

**9 WORDS**

What is an 'escutcheon'?
- a) a blunt instrument
- b) a shield
- c) a helmet

**10 POT LUCK**

On what date is Bastille Day celebrated in France?

ANSWERS ON PAGE 263

# QUIZ 50

**1  MOVIES**
Jeff Goldblum and Geena Davis starred in a 1980s remake of which 1950s horror movie?

**2  MUSIC**
Who composed the operas *Rigoletto*, *Aïda* and *Il Trovatore*?

**3  TV AND RADIO**
Which TV series follows the aftermath of the crash of Oceanic flight 815?

**4  SPORT AND LEISURE**
Which Celtic sport is regulated by the Camanachd Association?

**5  HISTORY**
Which queen of the Iceni led an unsuccessful revolt against the Romans in England in AD 60?

**6  SCIENCE AND NATURE**
Crick and Watson are generally credited with discovering the structure of what in 1953?

**7  LITERATURE**
Who was Captain W E Johns's famous literary aviator hero?

**8  CELEBRITIES**
What was the name of Jennifer Aniston and Vince Vaughn's 2006 anti-romantic movie comedy?

**9  WORDS**
What is a 'telpherage'?
        a) a tax on fruit
        b) an overhead transport system
        c) a religious office

**10  POT LUCK**
Which Italian dramatist wrote *Can't Pay! Won't Pay!* and *Accidental Death of an Anarchist*?

ANSWERS ON PAGE 263

# QUIZ 51

**1  MOVIES**
In 2001, Emily Watson, Helen Mirren, Kristin Scott Thomas, Alan Bates and Stephen Fry all starred in which Robert Altman movie?

**2  MUSIC**
What is the name of the lead singer of the Happy Mondays and Black Grape?

**3  TV AND RADIO**
Hosted by Pete Murray, Judith Chalmers, Terry Wogan, Angela Rippon and many others, which BBC TV series ran from 1949 to 1995?

**4  SPORT AND LEISURE**
In yachting, how frequently is the Admiral's Cup usually held?

**5  HISTORY**
Of which country did Lech Walesa become president in 1990?

**6  GEOGRAPHY**
Which meteorological sea area has borders with Forties, Tyne, Humber and German Bight?

**7  LITERATURE**
Which bestselling author's books include *The Horse Whisperer*, *The Loop*, *The Smoke Jumper* and *The Divide*?

**8  SCIENCE AND NATURE**
An amalgam is an alloy of which element and any other metal?

**9  WORDS**
What is a 'quagga'?
> a) an extinct zebra-like animal
> b) a fizzy white wine
> c) a tree with two boles

**10  POT LUCK**
In Chinese reckoning, the years 1940, 1952, 1964, 1976, 1988 and 2000 were linked to which animal?

ANSWERS ON PAGE 263

# QUIZ 52

**1 MOVIES**

Dennis Hopper, Isabella Rossellini and Laura Dern all starred in which unsettling 1980s David Lynch movie?

**2 MUSIC**

'Tears' was a 1965 Number One for which singer, better known as a comedian?

**3 TV AND RADIO**

Who was the original presenter of BBC1's *Question Time*?

**4 SPORT AND LEISURE**

Which sport is played by the LA Lakers, the Chicago Bulls and the New York Knicks?

**5 HISTORY**

Which US aviator completed the first non-stop solo transatlantic flight in 1927?

**6 SCIENCE AND NATURE**

With what essential medical invention is French physician René Laënnec credited?

**7 LITERATURE**

Who wrote the novel *Les Misérables*?

**8 CELEBRITIES**

Which Warren Beatty movie starred Madonna as a character called Breathless Mahoney?

**9 WORDS**

What is 'badderlock'?

- a) a seaweed
- b) an outdated swear word
- c) an Austrian prison

**10 POT LUCK**

In which war did Florence Nightingale volunteer for duty?

ANSWERS ON PAGE 263

# QUIZ 53

**1 MOVIES**
Minnie Driver starred with Matt Damon and Ben Affleck in which Oscar-winning movie of 1997?

**2 MUSIC**
Which revered country singer featured on the KLF's 1991 single 'Justified and Ancient'?

**3 TV AND RADIO**
Lee Majors starred as stuntman Colt Seavers in which television series?

**4 SPORT AND LEISURE**
Which country hosted the first World Cup competition in 1930?

**5 HISTORY**
Who was the Lord Protector of England from 1653 to 1658?

**6 GEOGRAPHY**
The Golden Gate Bridge is a feature of which US city?

**7 LITERATURE**
Which English author wrote the acclaimed children's trilogy *His Dark Materials*?

**8 SCIENCE AND NATURE**
Litmus turns red in the presence of what?

**9 WORDS**
Which toy is thought to derive its name from a Filipino word for a weapon?
- a) top
- b) frisbee
- c) yo-yo

**10 POT LUCK**
Where on your body would you wear a kepi?

ANSWERS ON PAGE 263

# QUIZ 54

**1 MOVIES**

In which musical did Doris Day sing 'Deadwood Stage', 'Windy City' and 'Secret Love'?

**2 MUSIC**

Who has been Queen's lead guitarist since the band's inception?

**3 TV AND RADIO**

Joanne Whalley played Bob Peck's murdered daughter in which seminal 1980s BBC thriller?

**4 SPORT AND LEISURE**

Who won the football World Cup in 2006?

**5 HISTORY**

Which Italian fascist leader came to power in 1922?

**6 SCIENCE AND NATURE**

What does an anemometer measure the speed of?

**7 LITERATURE**

What is 'Red October' in Tom Clancy's book *The Hunt for Red October*?

**8 CELEBRITIES**

Brad Pitt and Angelina Jolie starred as unhappily married assassins in which movie?

**9 WORDS**

A 'shadoof' is a mechanism for raising what?
> a) walls
> b) water
> c) logs

**10 POT LUCK**

Of which country is Hanoi the capital city?

ANSWERS ON PAGE 263

# QUIZ 55

**1 MOVIES**

Beatrice Dalle starred in a famous 1986 French movie called *37°2 Le Matin*. What was its English title?

**2 MUSIC**

Which legendary blues singer, dead before he was 30, wrote 'Sweet Home Chicago' and 'Hellhound on My Trail'?

**3 TV AND RADIO**

Which TV trivia quiz did Noel Edmonds host from 1985 to 1998?

**4 SPORT AND LEISURE**

Where have the TT races been held since 1909?

**5 HISTORY**

Which country was once ruled by the Tokugawa Shogunate?

**6 GEOGRAPHY**

The line of 0° longitude famously passes through which London borough?

**7 LITERATURE**

Which broadcaster has published novels including *The Last Lighthouse Keeper* and autobiographical books including *Trowel and Error*?

**8 SCIENCE AND NATURE**

Which pioneering scientist won the Nobel prize for chemistry in 1911, having isolated pure radium the year before?

**9 WORDS**

What does 'pellucid' mean?
- a) dangerous
- b) transparent
- c) having three feet

**10 POT LUCK**

What is the astrological birth sign of someone born on St George's Day?

ANSWERS ON PAGE 264

# QUIZ 56

**1 MOVIES**

Jeff Goldblum, Sigourney Weaver and Christopher Walken all had brief early roles in which Woody Allen movie?

**2 MUSIC**

Who sang with Van Morrison on the single 'Whenever God Shines his Light'?

**3 TV AND RADIO**

Which zoo-based BBC sitcom stars Julian Barratt and Noel Fielding?

**4 SPORT AND LEISURE**

The movie *Hurricane* was about which boxer?

**5 GEOGRAPHY**

Of which north-west African republic is Nouakchott the capital city?

**6 SCIENCE AND NATURE**

The Earth has a molten core mainly composed of nickel and which other metal?

**7 ART**

Which British writer and artist illustrated his own work *Songs of Innocence and Experience*?

**8 CELEBRITIES**

For which movie did Hilary Swank win her Oscar for Best Actress?

**9 WORDS**

Who would someone have killed in the act of 'uxoricide'?
- a) his wife
- b) his mother
- c) his daughter

**10 POT LUCK**

'Myrmecology' is the study of which animals?

ANSWERS ON PAGE 264

# QUIZ 57

**1  MOVIES**
What is the name of the cowboy voiced by Tom Hanks in the *Toy Story* movies?

**2  MUSIC**
Which *Blue Peter* presenter of the 1980s is the mother of singer Sophie Ellis-Bextor?

**3  TV AND RADIO**
Tony Hart, Wilf Lunn, Pat Keysall and Sylvester McCoy starred in which BBC show originally devised for people with hearing disabilities?

**4  SPORT AND LEISURE**
Who was the World Professional Darts champion from 1980 to 1981 and 1984 to 1986?

**5  HISTORY**
In which year was John Lennon killed?

**6  GEOGRAPHY**
Kigali is the capital of which African country?

**7  LITERATURE**
The book *Porno* is a sequel to which influential Scottish novel of the 1990s?

**8  SCIENCE AND NATURE**
When something undergoes galvanization, with what does it become coated?

**9  WORDS**
What does 'vermiform' mean?
> a) truthful
> b) decorative
> c) wormlike

**10  POT LUCK**
In heraldry, what colour is 'gules'?

ANSWERS ON PAGE 264

# QUIZ 58

**1 MOVIES**
James Dean, Natalie Wood and Sal Mineo starred in which classic 1950s Nicholas Ray movie?

**2 MUSIC**
Who composed the 'Brandenburg Concertos'?

**3 TV AND RADIO**
Which *Eastenders* character was played by Danniella Westbrook?

**4 SPORT AND LEISURE**
How many pawns are on the board at the beginning of a chess game?

**5 HISTORY**
Who was the queen of the Netherlands from 1948 to 1980?

**6 SCIENCE AND NATURE**
Which Cumbrian plutonium production reactor suffered a catastrophic fire in 1957?

**7 LITERATURE**
How is the Leslie Charteris character Simon Templar better known?

**8 CELEBRITIES**
Who is the famous footballing father of Gabby Logan?

**9 WORDS**
Where does a 'holobenthic' creature complete its lifecycle?
- a) an elephant's graveyard
- b) deep under the ocean
- c) up a tree

**10 POT LUCK**
Who wrote the plays *The Cocktail Party* and *Murder in the Cathedral*?

ANSWERS ON PAGE 264

# QUIZ 59

**1 MOVIES**
Kathleen Turner starred with Jack Nicholson in which John Huston gangster film of 1985?

**2 MUSIC**
What, according to The Buggles's 1979 hit, did video kill?

**3 TV AND RADIO**
Who played Jim Rockford in *The Rockford Files*?

**4 SPORT AND LEISURE**
Of which sport was Kelly Slater the world champion from 1994 to 1998?

**5 HISTORY**
In which year was the Falklands War?

**6 GEOGRAPHY**
Of which island is Palermo the capital?

**7 LITERATURE**
*Stranger Than Fiction* is Michael Crick's biography of which colourful political character?

**8 SCIENCE AND NATURE**
What is the yellow mineral iron pyrites commonly known as?

**9 WORDS**
What does 'plangent' mean?
- a) hard and woody
- b) deep and resonant
- c) light and funny

**10 POT LUCK**
With which berry is the spirit gin flavoured?

ANSWERS ON PAGE 264

# QUIZ 60

**1 MOVIES**
Which journalist has been played in movies by Margot Kidder and Kate Bosworth?

**2 MUSIC**
What was John Lennon's last solo UK Number One hit?

**3 TV AND RADIO**
Which Hawaii-based private eye was played by Tom Selleck?

**4 SPORT AND LEISURE**
In Rugby Union, which country joined five others in 2000 to participate in the renamed Six Nations championship?

**5 GEOGRAPHY**
What is the sea passage between Russia and Alaska called?

**6 SCIENCE AND NATURE**
What is the name given to the luminous atmospheric phenomena of the southern hemisphere?

**7 ART**
Which Dutch artist painted *Starry Night* and *Self-Portrait with Bandaged Ear*?

**8 CELEBRITIES**
Who or what was Max, long-time companion of the actor George Clooney?

**9 WORDS**
What is a 'reticule'?
- a) a net bag
- b) a steady income
- c) a group of followers

**10 POT LUCK**
What was the name of the South African jail in which Nelson Mandela was imprisoned for 18 years from 1964 to 1982?

ANSWERS ON PAGE 264

# QUIZ 61

**1 MOVIES**

Lauren Bacall became the fourth wife of which of her co-stars in *To Have And Have Not*?

**2 MUSIC**

Rossini's *William Tell* overture is well-known as the theme tune of which vintage TV series?

**3 TV AND RADIO**

What are the first names of Little and Large?

**4 SPORT AND LEISURE**

Which American football match takes place each January between the winners of the American Football Conference and the National Football Conference?

**5 HISTORY**

Who succeeded Winston Churchill as the British prime minister in 1945?

**6 GEOGRAPHY**

Which US state is known as the 'Bluegrass state'?

**7 LITERATURE**

Which comedian wrote the novels *Stark, Inconceivable* and *Dead Famous*?

**8 SCIENCE AND NATURE**

What is the symbol for silver as a chemical element?

**9 WORDS**

A 'googol' is a one followed by what?

        a) 100 zeros

        b) 1,000 zeros

        c) 1,000,000 zeros

**10 POT LUCK**

Which football manager was the co-creator of the 1970s TV series *Hazell*?

ANSWERS ON PAGE 265

# QUIZ 62

**1 MOVIES**
Carrie Fisher and Twiggy both had cameo roles in which John Belushi and Dan Aykroyd musical comedy?

**2 MUSIC**
Who had hits with 'My Old Man's a Dustman' and 'Does Your Chewing Gum Lose its Flavour on the Bedpost Overnight'?

**3 TV AND RADIO**
The Soup Dragon was a neighbour of which TV space-dwelling puppets?

**4 SPORT AND LEISURE**
In which sport is a 'niblick' used?

**5 HISTORY**
Who was the Japanese emperor from 1926 to 1989?

**6 SCIENCE AND NATURE**
The adult male of which bird is called a cob?

**7 LITERATURE**
Who wrote *The Private Memoirs and Confessions of a Justified Sinner*?

**8 CELEBRITIES**
Which filmmaker was married to both Jane Fonda and Brigitte Bardot?

**9 WORDS**
Where would you find a 'quillon'?
      a) in soup
      b) on a sword handle
      c) in a supernova

**10 POT LUCK**
Which ground is the headquarters of Surrey County Cricket Club?

ANSWERS ON PAGE 265

# QUIZ 63

**1 MOVIES**
In which 1960s sci-fi classic do Raquel Welch and Donald Pleasence pilot a miniaturized submarine inside a man's body?

**2 MUSIC**
Which legendary British musician was behind the 1980s movie musical *Give My Regards to Broad Street*?

**3 TV AND RADIO**
What number was the green Thunderbird in *Thunderbirds*?

**4 SPORT AND LEISURE**
Which Fijian golf player won the US Masters in 2000?

**5 HISTORY**
Which English king had the nicknames 'Longshanks' and 'the Hammer of the Scots'?

**6 GEOGRAPHY**
By what name was the country of Myanmar previously known?

**7 LITERATURE**
Which British writer was played by Anthony Hopkins in the movie *Shadowlands*?

**8 SCIENCE AND NATURE**
What lies at the centre of the heliocentric model of the solar system?

**9 WORDS**
The word 'cetacean' describes which animals?
- a) vultures
- b) whales
- c) wolves

**10 POT LUCK**
Which sports commentator turned guru has written books called *The Robots' Rebellion* and *Truth Vibrations*?

ANSWERS ON PAGE 265

# QUIZ 64

**1 MOVIES**
Who played the Limey in Steven Soderbergh's movie of the same name?

**2 MUSIC**
'I Owe You Nothing' was the only UK Number One for which 1980s boy band?

**3 TV AND RADIO**
Which 1970s TV series, set during World War II, was based on a biographical book by Major Pat Reid?

**4 SPORT AND LEISURE**
Which Scunthorpe-born golfer scored a famous hole-in-one in the 1967 Dunlop Masters?

**5 HISTORY**
From 1739 to 1743, the War of Jenkins' Ear was fought between Britain and which other nation?

**6 SCIENCE AND NATURE**
Camargue bulls and horses come from a delta region in which country?

**7 LITERATURE**
Julie Christie starred in a Truffaut movie adaptation of which Ray Bradbury novel?

**8 CELEBRITIES**
Who is Zara Phillips's mother?

**9 WORDS**
What is a 'coypu'?
- a) a Russian spacecraft
- b) an African vegetable
- c) a South American rodent

**10 POT LUCK**
Charon was the mythological ferryman on the Acheron and which other river?

ANSWERS ON PAGE 265

# QUIZ 65

**1   MOVIES**
Brad Pitt, Edward Norton and Helena Bonham Carter starred in which violent movie of 1999?

**2   MUSIC**
Who was the guitarist and vocalist with the 1960s supergroup Cream?

**3   TV AND RADIO**
Originally called David White, this man starred in *Open All Hours* and was knighted in 2005. By what name do we know him?

**4   SPORT AND LEISURE**
Brian Jacks rose to fame in 1970s sports show *Superstars* but at which sport did he famously compete?

**5   HISTORY**
The Spanish Civil War took place in which decade of the 20th century?

**6   GEOGRAPHY**
Port-au-Prince is the capital of which country?

**7   LITERATURE**
Which Russian novelist wrote the classic *Crime and Punishment*?

**8   SCIENCE AND NATURE**
Which scientific subject did Margaret Thatcher study at Oxford?

**9   WORDS**
What is a 'nabob'?
   a) an important man
   b) a Scottish tramp
   c) a mill worker

**10   POT LUCK**
Who was the lead singer with Thin Lizzy?

ANSWERS ON PAGE 265

# QUIZ 66

**1  MOVIES**

Margaret Lockwood took to highway robbery in which 1940s movie, also starring James Mason?

**2  MUSIC**

In which year did Kylie Minogue's first single, 'I Should Be So Lucky', reach Number One in the UK?

**3  TV AND RADIO**

Who was the presenter of the long-running Channel 4 quiz *Fifteen To One*?

**4  SPORT AND LEISURE**

Which rugby player's last-minute drop goal secured England's victory over Australia in the 2003 World Cup?

**5  HISTORY**

The Greek sculptor Phidias was responsible for which of the Seven Wonders of the World?

**6  SCIENCE AND NATURE**

Into which vitamin does the liver convert carotene?

**7  LITERATURE**

Nero Wolfe was the creation of which crime writer?

**8  CELEBRITIES**

What instrument does Nicola Benedetti play?

**9  WORDS**

What is 'dornick'?
- a) a heavy cloth
- b) a mossy covering
- c) a goat's cheese

**10  POT LUCK**

In Roald Dahl's *Charlie and the Chocolate Factory*, what is Charlie's surname?

ANSWERS ON PAGE 265

# QUIZ 67

**1 MOVIES**

Samantha Mumba starred in a 2001 remake of which 1950s movie?

**2 MUSIC**

What was Beethoven's first name?

**3 TV AND RADIO**

Which famous bumbling TV conjuror, who died onstage in 1984, was born in Caerphilly?

**4 SPORT AND LEISURE**

Which Sheffield venue annually hosts the World Professional Snooker Championship?

**5 HISTORY**

Who was the US president from 1945 to 1953?

**6 GEOGRAPHY**

What is the world's second-highest mountain?

**7 LITERATURE**

Which of Salman Rushdie's novels won the Booker Prize in 1981?

**8 SCIENCE AND NATURE**

The mineral haematite is a chief source of which metal?

**9 WORDS**

The Greek word for 'gigantic statue' gives us which modern word meaning large?

    a) massive
    b) enormous
    c) colossal

**10 POT LUCK**

The *Veda* is the literature of which religion?

ANSWERS ON PAGE 266

# QUIZ 68

**1 MOVIES**
Hugh Jackman voiced Roddy and Kate Winslet voiced Rita in which animated film of 2006?

**2 MUSIC**
Jane Birkin had a hit in 1969 singing 'Je T'Aime ... Moi Non Plus' with which infamous French bon vivant?

**3 TV AND RADIO**
In which hard-hitting US cop TV series does Michael Chiklis play Detective Vic Mackey?

**4 SPORT AND LEISURE**
Which football team were runners-up in the 1974 World Cup?

**5 HISTORY**
Which king's reign immediately preceded that of Queen Victoria?

**6 SCIENCE AND NATURE**
What name is given to an aquatic burrowing and egg-laying Australian mammal with broadly-webbed feet and duck-like bill?

**7 LITERATURE**
Which science fiction author wrote the *Foundation* trilogy and *I, Robot*?

**8 CELEBRITIES**
What was James Dean's final film?

**9 WORDS**
'Fagaceous' is a word describing a particular family of what?
      a) trees
      b) mushrooms
      c) mammals

**10 POT LUCK**
Bucephalus was the horse of which legendary leader?

ANSWERS ON PAGE 266

# QUIZ 69

**1  MOVIES**
Peter O'Toole, Alec Guinness and Omar Sharif all starred in which Oscar-winning epic of 1962?

**2  MUSIC**
Which jazz musician composed the score for Michael Winner's 1974 movie *Death Wish*?

**3  TV AND RADIO**
Joanna Lumley appeared with David McCallum in which eerie ITV drama series about two paranormal investigators?

**4  SPORT AND LEISURE**
What is the name of the tree trunk traditionally tossed during Highland Games?

**5  HISTORY**
Which former New York City mayor related his 9/11 experiences in a book called *Leadership*?

**6  GEOGRAPHY**
Into which sea does the river Nile ultimately flow?

**7  LITERATURE**
*Jaws* was one of the bestselling novels of the 1970s. Who wrote it?

**8  SCIENCE AND NATURE**
In computing, what unit is made up of 1000 or 1024 bytes?

**9  WORDS**
What was a 'janissary'?
  a) a European mapmaker
  b) a Canadian preacher
  c) a Turkish infantryman

**10  POT LUCK**
What is the nationality of Erno Rubik, inventor of the Rubik Cube?

ANSWERS ON PAGE 266

# QUIZ 70

**1 MOVIES**

*Night of the Hunter* was the only film ever directed by which actor?

**2 MUSIC**

Corinne Bailey Rae and the Kaiser Chiefs both come from which city?

**3 TV AND RADIO**

Who played the scheming government whip Francis Urquhart in *House of Cards*?

**4 SPORT AND LEISURE**

Which tennis player beat John McEnroe in the 1980 Wimbledon men's singles final?

**5 HISTORY**

Which country did Britain fight in the Opium Wars of the 19th century?

**6 SCIENCE AND NATURE**

In astronomy, which creature is represented by the constellation Cygnus?

**7 LITERATURE**

Becky Sharp and Amelia Sedley are the heroines of which 19th-century novel?

**8 CELEBRITIES**

Rapper Kid Rock separated from which US actress in November 2006 after less than four months of marriage?

**9 WORDS**

To 'animadvert' is to what?
- a) enliven
- b) criticize
- c) deflect

**10 POT LUCK**

Of which country is William Tell the national hero?

ANSWERS ON PAGE 266

# QUIZ 71

**1 MOVIES**
Britt Ekland, Christopher Lee and Edward Woodward appeared in which classic British horror movie?

**2 MUSIC**
Who had a Number One hit in 1961 with 'Runaway'?

**3 TV AND RADIO**
Who hosted *Sale of the Century* on TV and chairs *Just a Minute* on Radio 4?

**4 SPORT AND LEISURE**
Which cricketer captained the West Indies to victory in the World Cup in both 1975 and 1979?

**5 HISTORY**
In which year did the French Revolution begin?

**6 GEOGRAPHY**
Which historic Pennsylvanian port is known as 'the city of brotherly love'?

**7 LITERATURE**
Which British science fiction author wrote *2001: A Space Odyssey*?

**8 SCIENCE AND NATURE**
Which engineer was responsible for building the Clifton Suspension Bridge in Bristol?

**9 WORDS**
What is a 'meniscus'?
    a) the curved surface of a liquid
    b) a sacrificial dagger
    c) a list of possible choices

**10 POT LUCK**
In US politics, the Democrats adopted the ass as the symbol of their party. Which animal did the Republicans adopt?

ANSWERS ON PAGE 266

# QUIZ 72

**1 MOVIES**
Julia Roberts, Kirsten Dunst and Maggie Gyllenhaal starred in which 2003 movie set in a US girls' college?

**2 MUSIC**
Which song was a posthumous UK hit for Nat King Cole in a duet with his daughter Natalie?

**3 TV AND RADIO**
Who presents the Channel 4 TV programme *Grand Designs*?

**4 SPORT AND LEISURE**
Which Scottish rally driver won the World Rally Championship in 1995?

**5 HISTORY**
Which US militant political organization was founded by Huey P Newton and Bobby Seale in 1966?

**6 SCIENCE AND NATURE**
Which element gets its name from the Greek word for hidden?

**7 LITERATURE**
What was the name of the Brontë sisters's brother?

**8 CELEBRITIES**
Maria Bello played Dr Anna Del Amico in which US television series?

**9 WORDS**
What is something 'auriform' shaped like?
    a) an ear
    b) a halo
    c) a gold nugget

**10 POT LUCK**
Tarragona is a wine region in which European country?

ANSWERS ON PAGE 266

# QUIZ 73

**1   MOVIES**
Sheryl Lee played which doomed character in the 1992 film *Twin Peaks: Fire Walk with Me*?

**2   MUSIC**
Who had the original hit with 'I Love Rock 'n' Roll' in 1982?

**3   TV AND RADIO**
What was the name of Carla Lane's 1970s comedy starring Wendy Craig, Geoffrey Palmer and a very young Nicholas Lyndhurst?

**4   SPORT AND LEISURE**
Which football legend has managed Ipswich, PSV Eindhoven, Sporting Lisbon, Barcelona and Newcastle United in his career?

**5   HISTORY**
Who succeeded Queen Victoria in 1901?

**6   GEOGRAPHY**
Bridgetown is the capital city of which island?

**7   LITERATURE**
What is the name of the US satirist whose book *Stupid White Men* became a bestseller in 2002?

**8   SCIENCE AND NATURE**
What do the letters LED stand for?

**9   WORDS**
The Italian words for 'beautiful lady' provide which deadly poison with its name?

**10   POT LUCK**
Approximately how many miles is the diameter of the Earth?
   a) 7,900
   b) 79,000
   c) 790,000

ANSWERS ON PAGE 267

# QUIZ 74

**1 MOVIES**
Woody Harrelson and Juliette Lewis played murderous couple Mickey and Mallory in which 1990s movie?

**2 MUSIC**
Which instrument does jazz musician Wynton Marsalis play?

**3 TV AND RADIO**
Who preceded Jeremy Paxman as presenter of *University Challenge*?

**4 SPORT AND LEISURE**
The 1993 film *Cool Runnings* was based upon the true story of a Jamaican team competing in which sport?

**5 GEOGRAPHY**
What is the name of the French national anthem?

**6 SCIENCE AND NATURE**
What value of a fabric, garment or quilt is a measure of its thermal insulating ability?

**7 LITERATURE**
Which Japanese novelist wrote *A Wild Sheep Chase*?

**8 CELEBRITIES**
Which actor played John Horatio Malkovich in the 1999 film *Being John Malkovich*?

**9 WORDS**
What sort of monster is a 'lycanthrope'?
- a) a vampire
- b) a werewolf
- c) a mummy

**10 POT LUCK**
On which day of the month are the ides of March, May, July and October?

ANSWERS ON PAGE 267

# QUIZ 75

**1  MOVIES**
Which Stephen King novel was filmed by Stanley Kubrick?

**2  MUSIC**
'Musclebound', 'Lifeline' and 'Communication' were all hits for which New Romantic band?

**3  TV AND RADIO**
In which TV series did Farrah Fawcett-Majors play Jill Munroe?

**4  SPORT AND LEISURE**
Which then tennis professional was cast as Vijay in the 1983 James Bond movie *Octopussy*?

**5  HISTORY**
What were Winston Churchill's middle names?

**6  GEOGRAPHY**
Which single word, from the Greek meaning having the feet opposite, might a Briton use to describe Australia?

**7  LITERATURE**
For which novel is Boris Pasternak mainly known?

**8  SCIENCE AND NATURE**
The name of which seabird is believed to come from the Old Norse meaning 'foul gull'?

**9  WORDS**
Which word is repeated randomly by actors to simulate the sound of conversation?
    a) hubble
    b) cupboard
    c) rhubarb

**10  POT LUCK**
Which paper size is twice as large as A4?

ANSWERS ON PAGE 267

# QUIZ 76

**1 MOVIES**
Christian Bale, John Malkovich and Miranda Richardson all starred in which Spielberg film?

**2 MUSIC**
'September' and 'Boogie Wonderland' were 1970s disco hits for which band?

**3 TV AND RADIO**
Which comedian originally hosted the TV quiz *Winner Takes All*?

**4 SPORT AND LEISURE**
Which British woman athlete earned a gold medal for the 400m hurdles at the 1992 Barcelona Olympics?

**5 HISTORY**
Which monarch was the first of the House of Plantagenet?

**6 SCIENCE AND NATURE**
What did the Manhattan Project in the USA secretly attempt to engineer?

**7 LITERATURE**
Laurence Olivier and Joan Fontaine starred in a movie adaptation of which Daphne Du Maurier novel?

**8 CELEBRITIES**
Of which BBC TV science show did Carol Vorderman become a presenter in 1994?

**9 WORDS**
If you 'enervate' someone what do you do to them?
    a) thrill them
    b) terrify them
    c) weaken them

**10 POT LUCK**
Which steam organ takes its name from the Greek muse of epic poetry?

ANSWERS ON PAGE 267

# QUIZ 77

**1 MOVIES**

Which actor connects the Hitchcock movies *Vertigo, Rope* and *Rear Window*?

**2 MUSIC**

How would a musical passage marked 'accelerando' be played?

**3 TV AND RADIO**

Which English businessman and entrepreneur is featured in the BBC series *The Apprentice*?

**4 SPORT AND LEISURE**

Which US boxer was the world heavyweight champion from 1962 to 1964?

**5 HISTORY**

What was the name of the US spyplane pilot shot down and captured by the Soviets in 1960?

**6 GEOGRAPHY**

Africa's fourth-longest river originates in north-west Zambia and flows 1,700 miles to the Indian Ocean. What is it called?

**7 LITERATURE**

Who writes the *Dalziel and Pascoe* novels?

**8 SCIENCE AND NATURE**

What was the name of the comet that came within 125 million miles of Earth in 1997, becoming visible to the naked eye?

**9 WORDS**

Which breed of dog originally gets its name from a German word meaning to paddle or splash?
- a) poodle
- b) dachshund
- c) doberman

**10 POT LUCK**

On which Shakespeare play is *West Side Story* based?

ANSWERS ON PAGE 267

# QUIZ 78

**1 MOVIES**

Which actress first became famous for her role in *Bend It Like Beckham* in 2002 and went on to swashbuckle her way round the Caribbean?

**2 MUSIC**

What electronic musical instrument is played by moving the hands around antennae to vary pitch and volume?

**3 TV AND RADIO**

Avon, Vila and Servalan were characters in which BBC sci-fi TV series?

**4 SPORT AND LEISURE**

Which 24-hour motor race was first held in 1923?

**5 HISTORY**

In 1991, who became the first Briton in space?

**6 SCIENCE AND NATURE**

What is produced in the process of 'saponification'?

**7 LITERATURE**

Who wrote *The Old Man and the Sea* and *For Whom the Bell Tolls*?

**8 CELEBRITIES**

Which US actor's long-term partner is the French singer Vanessa Paradis?

**9 WORDS**

What is a 'vexillologist' interested in?
- a) umbrellas
- b) hats
- c) flags

**10 POT LUCK**

For which 1986 animated feature film did Eric Idle, Orson Welles and Leonard Nimoy provide voices?

ANSWERS ON PAGE 267

# QUIZ 79

**1 MOVIES**
How many Best Director Oscars did Alfred Hitchcock win?

**2 MUSIC**
Who had a hit with 'Under the Moon of Love' in 1976?

**3 TV AND RADIO**
Konnie Huq is a regular host on which BBC1 programme?

**4 SPORT AND LEISURE**
In which year was *Bluebird*-driver Donald Campbell killed?

**5 HISTORY**
Which celebrated British artist did crime writer Patricia Cornwell claim to have identified as Jack the Ripper?

**6 GEOGRAPHY**
Which island was formerly known as Van Diemen's Land?

**7 LITERATURE**
Michael Caine played Harry Palmer in *Funeral in Berlin* and *The Ipcress File*, but who wrote the books on which the films were based?

**8 SCIENCE AND NATURE**
How long is the cycle of sunspot activity?

**9 WORDS**
Which weapon gets its name from the Latin word for 'cramp-fish'?
        a) torpedo
        b) harpoon
        c) trident

**10 POT LUCK**
Rock band Jethro Tull took their name from an 18th-century English agriculturist. What was he famous for having invented?

ANSWERS ON PAGE 268

# QUIZ 80

**1  MOVIES**
Mike Leigh's 1999 movie *Topsy Turvy* was about which composers?

**2  MUSIC**
Which comedian had a novelty Number One hit about a milkman called Ernie?

**3  TV AND RADIO**
In which hard-hitting 1980s TV drama series did Bernard Hill play Yosser Hughes?

**4  SPORT AND LEISURE**
Which British athlete claimed that the decathlon was 'nine Mickey Mouse events and the 1500 metres'?

**5  GEOGRAPHY**
By which country is the republic of San Marino completely surrounded?

**6  SCIENCE AND NATURE**
To which body in the solar system is Nasa's spacecraft New Horizons on a mission?

**7  LITERATURE**
On whose original novel was the Myrna Loy and Dick Powell *Thin Man* series of films based?

**8  CELEBRITIES**
Which optical instrument is mentioned in the title of a 2004 album by K T Tunstall?

**9  WORDS**
What is 'legerdemain'?
> a) legal argument
> b) sleight of hand
> c) book-keeping

**10  POT LUCK**
What stage name did the illusionist Ehrich Weiss adopt?

ANSWERS ON PAGE 268

# QUIZ 81

**1 MOVIES**
Carrie-Anne Moss starred in which 1999 blockbuster and its two sequels in 2003?

**2 MUSIC**
Which jazz singer, originally called Eleanora Fagan, was nicknamed 'Lady Day'?

**3 TV AND RADIO**
What was the name of the owl in cult kids' TV programme *The Herbs*?

**4 SPORT AND LEISURE**
The 'oche' features in which sport?

**5 HISTORY**
Which Christian Greek-speaking empire, founded by the Roman emperor Constantine I in AD 330, thrived until 1453?

**6 GEOGRAPHY**
Which country is known by its inhabitants as Magyarország?

**7 LITERATURE**
Who wrote the original Tarzan novels?

**8 SCIENCE AND NATURE**
Do stalagmites grow up or hang down?

**9 WORDS**
'Defenestration' means throwing someone from what?
    a) a window
    b) a train
    c) a staircase

**10 POT LUCK**
Which politician and media star chose a large pot of French mustard as his luxury on *Desert Island Discs*?

ANSWERS ON PAGE 268

# QUIZ 82

**1  MOVIES**
Who directed and starred in the movie *The Three Burials of Melquiades Estrada*?

**2  MUSIC**
What was Unit Four Plus Two's only UK Number One?

**3  TV AND RADIO**
What is the name of John Nettles's character in *Midsomer Murders*?

**4  SPORT AND LEISURE**
Which controversial South African cricketer died in a plane crash in June 2002?

**5  HISTORY**
The Punic wars were waged between Rome and which other city state?

**6  SCIENCE AND NATURE**
How many faces are there on a tetrahedron?

**7  LITERATURE**
What was Inspector Morse's first name finally revealed to be?

**8  CELEBRITIES**
Bryce Dallas Howard is the daughter of which *Happy Days* star?

**9  WORDS**
If someone is 'gnathonic', what are they?
> a) inscrutable
> b) thin-limbed
> c) sycophantic

**10  POT LUCK**
In US slang, how much money is a 'sawbuck'?

ANSWERS ON PAGE 268

# QUIZ 83

**1 MOVIES**

The director of such films as *Plan 9 from Outer Space* and *Glen or Glenda* was himself the subject of a 1994 Tim Burton movie. What was his name?

**2 MUSIC**

Who wrote the 'Trout Quintet'?

**3 TV AND RADIO**

Miranda Richardson starred as Queen Elizabeth I in which 1980s BBC TV series?

**4 SPORT AND LEISURE**

Jean-Philippe Gatien and Jorgen Persson have been world champions in which sport?

**5 HISTORY**

Hitler's deputy flew to Scotland in 1941 in a one-man attempt to negotiate peace with Britain. What was his name?

**6 GEOGRAPHY**

Nassau is the capital of which 700-island archipelago?

**7 LITERATURE**

What was Margaret Mitchell's most famous book?

**8 SCIENCE AND NATURE**

Which 18th-century English chemist is credited with the discovery of oxygen?

**9 WORDS**

What is a 'godwit'?
- a) an idiot
- b) a bird
- c) a holy man

**10 POT LUCK**

Mossad is the intelligence service of which country?

ANSWERS ON PAGE 268

# QUIZ 84

**1   MOVIES**
Faye Dunaway and Warren Beatty starred as which pair of movie criminals in 1967?

**2   MUSIC**
Which Rolling Stone had a solo hit with 'Je Suis un Rock Star'?

**3   TV AND RADIO**
In which 1970s TV show did Patrick Duffy play a half-man, half-fish?

**4   SPORT AND LEISURE**
Where in the USA did the 2002 Winter Olympics take place?

**5   GEOGRAPHY**
How many major islands make up the Greek Dodecanese island group?

**6   SCIENCE AND NATURE**
The strandwolf is a species of which animal?

**7   LITERATURE**
Who was the most borrowed author from UK libraries in 2002–3, 2003–4, 2004–5 and 2005–6?

**8   CELEBRITIES**
To which TV presenter is Tess Daly married?

**9   WORDS**
What is 'strappado'?
>           a) a form of torture
>           b) a musical tempo
>           c) a display of temper

**10   POT LUCK**
What liquid measure is equal to four gills?

ANSWERS ON PAGE 268

# QUIZ 85

**1  MOVIES**
Ingrid Pitt starred in *Countess Dracula and the Vampire Lovers* for which legendary British film company?

**2  MUSIC**
Who recorded the landmark album *Blood on the Tracks* in 1975?

**3  TV AND RADIO**
Which Channel 4 TV show features 'the Queens of Clean', Kim and Aggie?

**4  SPORT AND LEISURE**
What is the maximum break possible in snooker?

**5  HISTORY**
Which popular uprising was led by Wat Tyler in 1381?

**6  GEOGRAPHY**
Where, north of the Arctic circle, would you find Thule, Dundas and Scoresbysund?

**7  LITERATURE**
Which singer published a book subtitled *La La La* in 2002?

**8  SCIENCE AND NATURE**
Where are the sphenoid, ethmoid and occipital bones?

**9  WORDS**
What is a 'strabismus' better known as?
- a) a stomach ache
- b) a limp
- c) a squint

**10  POT LUCK**
In British road signs, warnings are generally what shape?

ANSWERS ON PAGE 269

# QUIZ 86

**1 MOVIES**
In which movie was Kim Basinger the Bond girl?

**2 MUSIC**
Who had Top Ten hits with 'Vienna' and 'Dancing with Tears in My Eyes'?

**3 TV AND RADIO**
What is the top prize in the Noel Edmonds game show *Deal or No Deal*?

**4 SPORT AND LEISURE**
In which year was American Football's Super Bowl first held?

**5 HISTORY**
Which attempt to destroy the English parliament failed in 1605?

**6 SCIENCE AND NATURE**
The sclera is the covering of which part of the body?

**7 LITERATURE**
Who wrote the *Father Brown* mysteries?

**8 CELEBRITIES**
Sienna Miller starred with Jude Law in which remake of a 1960s Michael Caine movie?

**9 WORDS**
What is a 'numnah'?
- a) a saddle pad
- b) old Persian ruler
- c) a unit of currency

**10 POT LUCK**
Which Scottish author is featured on banknotes issued by the Bank of Scotland?

ANSWERS ON PAGE 269

# QUIZ 87

**1 MOVIES**

Who played Harrison Ford's father in *Indiana Jones and the Last Crusade*?

**2 MUSIC**

Who had a novelty Number One hit with 'Cotton Eye Joe' in 1994?

**3 TV AND RADIO**

Which celebrity declared he would rather eat his own hair than go shopping with *What Not To Wear*'s Trinny and Susannah again?

**4 SPORT AND LEISURE**

Which male US tennis player was Wimbledon singles champion in 1974 and 1982?

**5 HISTORY**

What was the name of the conflict between England and France that ran from 1337 to 1453?

**6 GEOGRAPHY**

On which island would you find the tiny state of Brunei?

**7 LITERATURE**

Who wrote *The Three Musketeers*?

**8 SCIENCE AND NATURE**

Apollo, Camberwell beauty, peacock and morpho are all types of which insect?

**9 WORDS**

'Salary' is derived from the Latin word *salarium*, meaning the money Roman soldiers were given to buy a specific substance. What was it?

**10 POT LUCK**

Who was the Roman god of wine?

ANSWERS ON PAGE 269

# QUIZ 88

**1 MOVIES**

Grace Kelly starred in three Hitchcock movies – *Dial M for Murder*, *Rear Window* and which other?

**2 MUSIC**

What was the only UK Number One for Donna Summer?

**3 TV AND RADIO**

Pugh, Pugh, Barney McGrew, Cuthbert, Dibble and Grub were characters in which children's animated show?

**4 SPORT AND LEISURE**

What is the German Formula 1 Grand Prix circuit called?

**5 HISTORY**

Who became the first First Minister of Scotland in 1999?

**6 SCIENCE AND NATURE**

Which element is Henry Cavendish credited with discovering in 1766?

**7 LITERATURE**

Which Frank Richards literary character was also known as the 'fat owl of the Remove'?

**8 CELEBRITIES**

For which movie did Charlize Theron win her first Best Actress Oscar?

**9 WORDS**

If someone is 'feckless', what are they?
- a) weak
- b) evil
- c) intoxicated

**10 POT LUCK**

Which direction can also be called 'widdershins'?

ANSWERS ON PAGE 269

# QUIZ 89

**1  MOVIES**

Jacqueline Bisset starred with Nick Nolte in which 1977 adaptation of a Peter Benchley novel?

**2  MUSIC**

Which Beethoven symphony is known as the 'Pastoral'?

**3  TV AND RADIO**

Judd Hirsch, Christopher Lloyd, Andy Kaufman and Danny DeVito all starred in which US comedy of the 1970s and 1980s?

**4  SPORT AND LEISURE**

Which champion cyclist wrote a book about his recovery from cancer called *It's Not About the Bike*?

**5  HISTORY**

Which Indian prime minister was assassinated in 1984?

**6  GEOGRAPHY**

In which country would you find Utrecht, Haarlem and Eindhoven?

**7  LITERATURE**

Whose wife wrote a biography of him simply entitled *Billy*?

**8  SCIENCE AND NATURE**

What were the first names of aviation pioneers the Wright brothers?

**9  WORDS**

'Rhinoplasty' is surgery performed on what?
- a) the scalp
- b) the chest
- c) the nose

**10  POT LUCK**

What is the name of the famous US prison, originally opened as 'Mount Pleasant', located in Ossining, New York?

ANSWERS ON PAGE 269

# QUIZ 90

**1 MOVIES**
In which movie did Kathleen Turner voice cartoon character Jessica Rabbit?

**2 MUSIC**
What is Eminem's real name?

**3 TV AND RADIO**
Who played Hyacinth Bucket in the sitcom *Keeping Up Appearances*?

**4 SPORT AND LEISURE**
The 'Stableford System' is an alternative scoring scheme in which sport?

**5 GEOGRAPHY**
In which country would you find the cities of Faisalabad and Rawalpindi?

**6 SCIENCE AND NATURE**
Stannum is an obsolete name for which metal?

**7 LITERATURE**
By what name is writer Charles Lutwidge Dodgson better known?

**8 CELEBRITIES**
In which Mike Myers film did Beyoncé Knowles star as Foxxy Cleopatra?

**9 WORDS**
What is a 'charivari'?
- a) a black and white drawing
- b) a confused noise
- c) an Italian seafood dish

**10 POT LUCK**
Where would you find the Dewey Decimal classification system used?

ANSWERS ON PAGE 269

# QUIZ 91

**1 MOVIES**
Nicolas Cage, Sean Connery and Ed Harris starred in which 1990s blockbuster?

**2 MUSIC**
*Yoshimi Battles the Pink Robots* was a hit 2003 album for whom?

**3 TV AND RADIO**
Which Massachusetts-born presenter links *Masterchef* and *Through the Keyhole*?

**4 SPORT AND LEISURE**
Jackknife, swallow, swan and pike are types of what?

**5 HISTORY**
In which century was the Inquisition abolished?

**6 GEOGRAPHY**
How far ahead of GMT is Iraq?

**7 LITERATURE**
Heather Graham starred in *Killing Me Softly*, a 2002 movie adaptation of a novel by which British crime writer?

**8 SCIENCE AND NATURE**
How many horns would you have found on the head of a triceratops?

**9 WORDS**
What is a 'gallimaufry'?
> a) a potent drink
> b) a curved club
> c) a hotchpotch

**10 POT LUCK**
What is Jools Holland's real first name?

ANSWERS ON PAGE 270

# QUIZ 92

**1  MOVIES**
Will Smith, Martin Lawrence and Téa Leoni starred in which buddy-cop action movie?

**2  MUSIC**
What was Holly Valance's 2002 UK Number One hit?

**3  TV AND RADIO**
What was the surname of the Major in *Fawlty Towers*?

**4  SPORT AND LEISURE**
In 1995, which New Zealand All Black became the first player to score twelve Test match tries in a calendar year?

**5  GEOGRAPHY**
Zealand, Fyn and Lolland are islands belonging to which country?

**6  SCIENCE AND NATURE**
Heartsease is another name for which flower?

**7  ART**
Who painted the Pop Art pieces *Whaam!* and *As I Opened Fire*?

**8  CELEBRITIES**
Glenda Jackson, Helen Mirren and Anne-Marie Duff have all played which ruler on TV?

**9  WORDS**
'Marmoreal' relates to what?
  a) oranges
  b) monkeys
  c) marble

**10  POT LUCK**
The 19th-century British prime minister W E Gladstone was nicknamed 'G O M'. What does this stand for?

ANSWERS ON PAGE 270

# QUIZ 93

**1 MOVIES**
Who directed *The Magnificent Seven*?

**2 MUSIC**
'The Lion Sleeps Tonight' and 'Fantasy Island' were 1980s hits for which group?

**3 TV AND RADIO**
Lucy Davis, who played Dawn in *The Office*, is the daughter of which famous comedian?

**4 SPORT AND LEISURE**
At which event did Al Oerter win four consecutive Olympic gold medals between 1956 and 1968?

**5 HISTORY**
In 1917, which British soldier led Arab forces to capture Aqaba?

**6 GEOGRAPHY**
What is the capital city of Nepal?

**7 LITERATURE**
Who was the Scottish author of the much-filmed novel *The Thirty-Nine Steps*?

**8 SCIENCE AND NATURE**
What is the square root of 169?

**9 WORDS**
'Chthonic' means relating to what?
   a) Heaven
   b) the underworld
   c) the sun

**10 POT LUCK**
Ian Hislop is the editor of which fortnightly satirical magazine?

ANSWERS ON PAGE 270

# QUIZ 94

**1  MOVIES**
*A Cock and Bull Story*, featuring Steve Coogan and Gillian Anderson, was based on which Laurence Sterne novel?

**2  MUSIC**
What was the title of the December 2002 Number One hit for Girls Aloud?

**3  TV AND RADIO**
Which TV detective did *Perry Mason* star Raymond Burr also play?

**4  SPORT AND LEISURE**
At which racecourse does the Derby take place?

**5  HISTORY**
Which country has borders with Denmark, Belgium and Poland?

**6  GEOGRAPHY**
In which two countries is the Chihuahua desert?

**7  ART**
In which field of the arts are Ansel Adams, Helmut Newton and Annie Leibovitz best known?

**8  CELEBRITIES**
Claire Danes appeared with which comedian in the film version of his own novel *Shopgirl*?

**9  WORDS**
What is a 'bacchant'?
       a) a hand of cards
       b) a lengthy song
       c) a drunken reveller

**10  POT LUCK**
Duncan, Banquo and Macduff are characters in which Shakespeare play?

ANSWERS ON PAGE 270

# QUIZ 95

**1 MOVIES**

Sylvia Kristel, Burt Lancaster, Dean Martin, James Stewart, Jack Lemmon, Alain Delon, Charlton Heston, Myrna Loy and Linda Blair all starred in which movie series?

**2 MUSIC**

Which Ian Dury track knocked 'YMCA' by the Village People off the Number One spot?

**3 TV AND RADIO**

Who played Audrey fforbes-Hamilton in *To The Manor Born*?

**4 SPORT AND LEISURE**

In which year was Michael Schumacher born?

**5 HISTORY**

In 1973 the Cod War broke out between Britain and which other country?

**6 GEOGRAPHY**

Madagascar lies off the coast of which East African country?

**7 LITERATURE**

Who wrote *The End of the Affair* and *Brighton Rock*?

**8 SCIENCE AND NATURE**

What was invented by the British engineer Christopher Cockerell in 1955?

**9 WORDS**

From which language do we get the word 'smörgåsbord', meaning a mixture of savoury dishes?
- a) Finnish
- b) Swedish
- c) Norwegian

**10 POT LUCK**

Where is the 'dong' the unit of currency?

ANSWERS ON PAGE 270

# QUIZ 96

**1 MOVIES**

Kristin Scott Thomas and Robert Redford starred in a movie adaptation of which Nicholas Evans novel?

**2 MUSIC**

'Minuetto Allegretto' was a 1974 Top 20 hit for which litter-tidying novelty group?

**3 TV AND RADIO**

In the 1960s TV show *Belle and Sebastian*, what kind of animal was Belle?

**4 SPORT AND LEISURE**

How many points does the brown ball score in snooker?

**5 HISTORY**

Which Scottish clan was massacred at Glencoe in 1692?

**6 SCIENCE AND NATURE**

What are belemnites, goniatites, ammonites and trilobites?

**7 LITERATURE**

Which English author wrote the poem 'The Hunting of the Snark'?

**8 CELEBRITIES**

Eric Bana and Drew Barrymore starred in *Lucky You*, a film about which game?

**9 WORDS**

What is a 'thaumaturge'?
- a) a magician
- b) an irrepressible impulse
- c) a throat doctor

**10 POT LUCK**

In mythology, who was condemned by Zeus to bear the heavens on his shoulders?

ANSWERS ON PAGE 270

# QUIZ 97

**1 MOVIES**
Julianne Moore replaced whom as Clarice Starling in Ridley Scott's *Hannibal*?

**2 MUSIC**
Which US singer was born in El Centro, California, in 1946?

**3 TV AND RADIO**
In the late 1970s and early 1980s, which radio station broadcast on 275, 285 and Stereo VHF?

**4 SPORT AND LEISURE**
Who succeeded Howard Wilkinson as manager of Sunderland?

**5 HISTORY**
Boutros Boutros-Ghali was the UN Secretary-General from 1992 to 1996. What was his nationality?

**6 GEOGRAPHY**
What is the official language in Tunisia?

**7 LITERATURE**
*The Clan of the Cave Bear* and its four bestselling sequels were written by which author?

**8 SCIENCE AND NATURE**
In which century did the Lumière brothers first demonstrate public cinema?

**9 WORDS**
Which phrase describes an institution that appears strong but is in fact weak?
       a) white elephant
       b) paper tiger
       c) Trojan horse

**10 POT LUCK**
Which intrepid explorer's companions included Dale Arden and Dr Zarkov?

ANSWERS ON PAGE 271

# QUIZ 98

**1 MOVIES**

Franka Potente and Matt Damon star in movies about which renegade Robert Ludlum agent?

**2 MUSIC**

'The Devil Went Down' to which US state in the only Charlie Daniels Band UK hit of the 1970s?

**3 TV AND RADIO**

Who played Private Pike in *Dad's Army*?

**4 SPORT AND LEISURE**

Which is the only letter in a standard Scrabble® set to be represented on twelve tiles?

**5 HISTORY**

On which date in 1944 did the D-Day landings in Normandy begin?

**6 SCIENCE AND NATURE**

German astronomer Johann Galle first observed which planet in 1846?

**7 LITERATURE**

Which US poet wrote *The Bell Jar*?

**8 CELEBRITIES**

Clémence Poésy played Fleur Delacour in which wizard movie of 2005?

**9 WORDS**

What material must a xylophone be made of?
- a) plastic
- b) metal
- c) wood

**10 POT LUCK**

To which New York Yankees baseball player was Marilyn Monroe briefly married?

ANSWERS ON PAGE 271

# QUIZ 99

**1  MOVIES**
Who played the US president in the 1997 movie *Air Force One*?

**2  MUSIC**
Stevie Nicks was a vocalist with which group?

**3  TV AND RADIO**
What was the surname of Matt LeBlanc's character in *Friends*?

**4  SPORT AND LEISURE**
Which West Indies and Nottinghamshire cricketer scored a record 365 not out against Pakistan in the 1958 Test?

**5  HISTORY**
Which Boston Tea Party raider was the subject of a subsequent poem by Longfellow?

**6  GEOGRAPHY**
Of which country is Pyongyang the capital?

**7  LITERATURE**
Who wrote *Homage to Catalonia, Down and Out in Paris and London* and *The Road to Wigan Pier*?

**8  SCIENCE AND NATURE**
Which British physicist discovered electromagnetic induction and the laws of electrolysis?

**9  WORDS**
'Flagellation' is what sort of punishment?
        a) whipping
        b) imprisonment
        c) fine

**10  POT LUCK**
What instrument does the leader of an orchestra play?

ANSWERS ON PAGE 271

# QUIZ 100

**1 MOVIES**

Jane Fonda starred as which AD 40,000 space heroine in a 1960s movie of the same name?

**2 MUSIC**

'Sailing', 'Baby Jane' and 'Da Ya Think I'm Sexy?' were Number One hits for which singer?

**3 TV AND RADIO**

Which quiz show was first transmitted in the UK on 4 September 1998?

**4 SPORT AND LEISURE**

In equestrianism, by what single word is the horse's saddle, bridle and bit known?

**5 HISTORY**

Which US battle is popularly known as 'Custer's Last Stand'?

**6 SCIENCE AND NATURE**

Which group of stars is colloquially known as the Crab?

**7 LITERATURE**

Who wrote *The Sign of Four*?

**8 CELEBRITIES**

Presenter Natasha Kaplinsky won the first series of which terpsichorean BBC TV reality show?

**9 WORDS**

How many sides does an 'icosahedron' have?

  a) 10
  b) 20
  c) 50

**10 POT LUCK**

In Britain, which Roman barrier ran from Wallsend in the east to Bowness on the Solway Firth in the west?

ANSWERS ON PAGE 271

# QUIZ 101

**1  MOVIES**
Uma Thurman starred in the two *Kill Bill* films in 2003 and 2004. Who was the director?

**2  MUSIC**
What was Wink Martindale's only UK hit?

**3  TV AND RADIO**
Gary Cole played Jack Killian in which TV show from the late 1980s and early 1990s?

**4  SPORT AND LEISURE**
Which Australian was the Formula 1 champion in 1959, 1960 and 1966?

**5  HISTORY**
In which battle did Davy Crockett die?

**6  GEOGRAPHY**
In India, one rupee is made up of 100 what?

**7  LITERATURE**
Who wrote *To Kill a Mockingbird*?

**8  SCIENCE AND NATURE**
Which meteorological phenomenon can be forked, sheet or ball?

**9  WORDS**
What does 'decimate' mean?
  a) to take or destroy 10 per cent of
  b) to take or destroy 50 per cent of
  c) to take or destroy 90 per cent of

**10  POT LUCK**
CH is the international car registration code for which country?

ANSWERS ON PAGE 271

# QUIZ 102

**1 MOVIES**

*Crouching Tiger, Hidden Dragon* star Michelle Yeoh was a Bond girl in which movie?

**2 MUSIC**

'Go', 'Hymn' and 'Porcelain' were three hits for which artist, originally named Richard Hall?

**3 TV AND RADIO**

Andy Sipowicz, Bobby Simone and Greg Medavoy were characters in which US police show?

**4 SPORT AND LEISURE**

Which German golfer was the first Number One when official rankings were introduced in 1986?

**5 GEOGRAPHY**

Which country was formerly known as Ceylon?

**6 SCIENCE AND NATURE**

How is 'light amplification by stimulated emission of radiation' usually abbreviated?

**7 LITERATURE**

Who wrote 'Ode to a Nightingale'?

**8 CELEBRITIES**

Rosamund Pike starred with the Rock in a movie adaptation of which computer game?

**9 WORDS**

What is a 'minuend'?
- a) a dance
- b) a mathematical term
- c) a unit of time

**10 POT LUCK**

Which gemstone is traditionally associated with the month of January?

ANSWERS ON PAGE 271

# QUIZ 103

**1 MOVIES**
In which classic 1966 movie did Raquel Welch star?

**2 MUSIC**
Which TV theme did punk band The Dickies cover in 1979?

**3 TV AND RADIO**
Which sports commentator also hosted BBC's *The Superstars* and *We are the Champions*?

**4 SPORT AND LEISURE**
In 1926 which baseball player became the first man to hit three home runs in one game?

**5 HISTORY**
Which Mongol people overran parts of the Roman empire in the 5th century under the leadership of Attila?

**6 GEOGRAPHY**
Arica, Valparaiso and Santiago are found in which country?

**7 LITERATURE**
Which Brontë sister wrote *The Tenant of Wildfell Hall* and *Agnes Grey*?

**8 SCIENCE AND NATURE**
How many bones are there in the human body?

**9 WORDS**
What is a 'trebuchet'?
        a) a toilet
        b) a garment
        c) a weapon

**10 POT LUCK**
In which country did Gruyère cheese originate?

ANSWERS ON PAGE 272

# QUIZ 104

**1  MOVIES**
Billie Whitelaw, Bernard Cribbins and Anna Massey starred in which Hitchcock film?

**2  MUSIC**
Which group recorded 'I'll Be There for You', the theme tune from the TV series *Friends*?

**3  TV AND RADIO**
What was the first name of the character played by Sarah Lancashire in *Coronation Street*?

**4  SPORT AND LEISURE**
Which boxer lost the British, European and Commonwealth heavyweight titles to Joe Bugner in 1971?

**5  HISTORY**
In AD 330, Constantinople became the capital of which empire?

**6  SCIENCE AND NATURE**
How is the table condiment composed of dilute acetic acid better known?

**7  LITERATURE**
Which otter did Henry Williamson write about?

**8  CELEBRITIES**
Halle Berry and Michelle Pfeiffer have both played which comic book character on the big screen?

**9  WORDS**
What is a 'zeugma'?
> a) an item of clothing
> b) a figure of speech
> c) a flight of fancy

**10  POT LUCK**
Which composer's last words are said to have been 'I shall hear in heaven'?

ANSWERS ON PAGE 272

# QUIZ 105

**1 MOVIES**

Whom did Charlie Chaplin satirize as Adenoid Hynkel in *The Great Dictator*?

**2 MUSIC**

Which controversial band charted with 'Love Missile F1-11' in 1986?

**3 TV AND RADIO**

Anna Friel played which character in *Brookside*?

**4 SPORT AND LEISURE**

Who was the world professional snooker champion from 1992 to 1996?

**5 HISTORY**

Who was the US president between Gerald Ford and Ronald Reagan?

**6 GEOGRAPHY**

The Tyrrhenian Sea lies off the west coast of which country?

**7 LITERATURE**

Who wrote the novel *Lolita*?

**8 SCIENCE AND NATURE**

The pneumatic tyre was invented in 1888 by which Scot?

**9 WORDS**

The disease 'framboesia', characterized by red swellings, gets its name from the French word for which fruit?
- a) raspberries
- b) strawberries
- c) cherries

**10 POT LUCK**

Which English film director, born in Leytonstone, East London, had cameo roles in most of his own films?

ANSWERS ON PAGE 272

# QUIZ 106

**1   MOVIES**
In which 1948 Humphrey Bogart film did Lauren Bacall play Nora Temple?

**2   MUSIC**
'Cats in the Cradle' was a 1990s UK Top Ten hit for which band?

**3   TV AND RADIO**
Who played Jim Rockford in the 1970s TV series *The Rockford Files*?

**4   SPORT AND LEISURE**
Former Manchester United goalkeeper Peter Schmeichel played for which national side?

**5   HISTORY**
Who led the Welsh rebellion against Henry IV in 1401?

**6   SCIENCE AND NATURE**
Which common drug was originally developed from the white willow?

**7   LITERATURE**
Who was Bertie Wooster's butler in the P G Wodehouse stories?

**8   CELEBRITIES**
Samantha Morton, Rosamund Pike and Johnny Depp featured in which biopic of the second Earl of Rochester?

**9   WORDS**
The 'manticore' had the head of a man and the body of a what?
  a) a horse
  b) a lion
  c) a bull

**10   POT LUCK**
A nebuchadnezzar is the equivalent of how many normal bottles of wine?

ANSWERS ON PAGE 272

# QUIZ 107

**1  MOVIES**
John Huston cast his daughter Anjelica as Maerose in which 1985 gangster movie?

**2  MUSIC**
What was the title of the 1972 Number One hit for the Pipes and Drums and Military Band of the Royal Scots Dragoon Guards?

**3  TV AND RADIO**
Which comedians originally played cops Dalziel and Pascoe, their run lasting only three episodes?

**4  SPORT AND LEISURE**
Which Swiss tennis player won the Wimbledon women's singles final in 1997?

**5  HISTORY**
In which year was the state of Israel established?

**6  GEOGRAPHY**
In which former Soviet republic is the city of Minsk?

**7  ART**
Where would you find the Prado Museum?

**8  SCIENCE AND NATURE**
From which plant is the drug digitalis derived?

**9  WORDS**
What does 'obsequious' mean?
> a) brown coloured
> b) drunk
> c) servile

**10  POT LUCK**
What is Smith and Wesson famous for manufacturing?

ANSWERS ON PAGE 272

# QUIZ 108

**1 MOVIES**
The 1980s Paul Newman movie *The Color of Money* was a sequel to which of his earlier films?

**2 MUSIC**
Christina Aguilera had a UK Number One in November 2002 with which song?

**3 TV AND RADIO**
Leonard Sachs was the wordy compère of which long-running TV music hall variety show?

**4 SPORT AND LEISURE**
William Webb Ellis reputedly invented which sport?

**5 HISTORY**
Which president abolished slavery in the USA in 1863?

**6 SCIENCE AND NATURE**
A tangram is a geometrical puzzle whose origin lies in which country?

**7 LITERATURE**
Who wrote the novel *The Little House on the Prairie*?

**8 CELEBRITIES**
Who was born in Leytonstone on 2 May 1975?

**9 WORDS**
What is someone who is 'gravid'?
- a) fat
- b) melancholy
- c) pregnant

**10 POT LUCK**
Who was the British prime minister before Margaret Thatcher won the 1979 election?

ANSWERS ON PAGE 272

# QUIZ 109

**1  MOVIES**
Faye Dunaway won the Best Actress Oscar for which 1976 movie satire of TV news broadcasting?

**2  MUSIC**
Which Manchester band's first hit was 'She Bangs the Drums' in 1989?

**3  TV AND RADIO**
In which prison was Norman Stanley Fletcher locked up?

**4  SPORT AND LEISURE**
Which English football team is nicknamed 'the Baggies'?

**5  HISTORY**
Which former president of Chile was arrested in Britain in 1998 for genocide?

**6  GEOGRAPHY**
Lilongwe is the capital of which African country?

**7  LITERATURE**
Arundhati Roy won the 1997 Booker Prize for which novel?

**8  SCIENCE AND NATURE**
What, specifically, do ungulates have that other animals do not?

**9  WORDS**
What is a 'cupola'?
- a) a small coffee
- b) a domed roof
- c) a European football competition

**10  POT LUCK**
Which volcano overwhelmed Herculaneum in AD 79?

ANSWERS ON PAGE 273

# QUIZ 110

**1   MOVIES**

In which 2005 movie did the daughter of Jodie Foster's character disappear on an aeroplane mid-flight?

**2   MUSIC**

Little Jimmy Osmond hit the Number One slot in 1972 as a 'Long Haired Lover' from where?

**3   TV AND RADIO**

What is the Christian name of the BBC news correspondent whose surname is Guerin?

**4   SPORT AND LEISURE**

Which Manchester United and French national football player received a ban for his kung fu attack on a Crystal Palace fan?

**5   GEOGRAPHY**

Lerwick is the most northerly town in the UK. On which island is it situated?

**6   SCIENCE AND NATURE**

What is the freezing point of water on the Fahrenheit temperature scale?

**7   LITERATURE**

In which Jane Austen novel would you encounter the Dashwood family?

**8   CELEBRITIES**

Fay Wray, Jessica Lange and Naomi Watts have all starred with which 'Eighth Wonder of the World'?

**9   WORDS**

What is 'somniloquence'?
- a) remarkable eloquence
- b) sleep-talking
- c) falling asleep whilst talking

**10   POT LUCK**

Which animal is represented by Capricorn?

ANSWERS ON PAGE 273

# QUIZ 111

**1 MOVIES**
Who plays the president in the 1993 movie *Dave*?

**2 MUSIC**
Whose albums include *Elite Hotel*, *Roses in the Snow* and *Wrecking Ball*?

**3 TV AND RADIO**
What was the name of Dennis Waterman's character in *Minder*?

**4 SPORT AND LEISURE**
Who earned 102 caps for Scotland's football team before going on to manage Liverpool, Blackburn Rovers and Newcastle United?

**5 HISTORY**
To which island was Napoleon exiled in 1814?

**6 GEOGRAPHY**
Which island in the Irish Sea has places called Port Erin and Kirk Michael?

**7 LITERATURE**
Who wrote *Watermelon*, *Lucy Sullivan is Getting Married* and *Sushi for Beginners*?

**8 SCIENCE AND NATURE**
Who invented the mercury thermometer in 1714?

**9 WORDS**
A 'hagiography' is an account of the life of whom?
        a) a criminal
        b) a saint
        c) a witch

**10 POT LUCK**
Which ingredient of guacamole gives it its distinctive green colour?

ANSWERS ON PAGE 273

# QUIZ 112

**1 MOVIES**
Rachel Weisz plays Ralph Fiennes' wife in which film adaptation of a John le Carré novel?

**2 MUSIC**
'Give It Away', 'Love Rollercoaster' and 'By the Way' were all UK Top Ten hits for which band?

**3 TV AND RADIO**
Which cockney comic played Wally Briggs in the TV series *Romany Jones* and *Yus My Dear*?

**4 SPORT AND LEISURE**
The ball burst in the 1946 FA Cup final between Charlton Athletic and which eventual winners?

**5 GEOGRAPHY**
Which US state is not in continental North America?

**6 SCIENCE AND NATURE**
Brock is another name for which animal?

**7 LITERATURE**
Jack Schaefer wrote which famous 1949 novel about an enigmatic cowboy?

**8 CELEBRITIES**
Catherine Zeta-Jones and Antonio Banderas have co-starred in films about which swashbuckling hero?

**9 WORDS**
What do you do at the end of the ritual of 'seppuku'?
- a) drink tea
- b) put your footwear back on
- c) die

**10 POT LUCK**
Whose head featured on the Penny Black postage stamp?

ANSWERS ON PAGE 273

# QUIZ 113

**1 MOVIES**
Who starred as Serpico in the 1970s movie of the same name?

**2 MUSIC**
What breakfast cereal-related chart hit did Tori Amos have in 1994?

**3 TV AND RADIO**
Which veteran English actress played the granny in *Metal Mickey*?

**4 SPORT AND LEISURE**
In which sport did Pat Eddery excel?

**5 HISTORY**
In 1976 Israeli commandos freed hostages from which Ugandan airport?

**6 GEOGRAPHY**
The island of Bermuda is found in which ocean?

**7 LITERATURE**
What was the title of Erich Maria Remarque's famous novel about World War I?

**8 SCIENCE AND NATURE**
How is the Sibbald's rorqual better known?

**9 WORDS**
What is an 'intaglio'?
- a) an ornamented gem
- b) a complicated situation
- c) a house of ill repute

**10 POT LUCK**
Who wrote the poem 'Do Not Go Gentle into That Good Night?'

ANSWERS ON PAGE 273

# QUIZ 114

**1 MOVIES**

Julia Roberts starred in which 1990s near-death experience movie with Kiefer Sutherland and Kevin Bacon?

**2 MUSIC**

If a musical piece is marked 'presto', at what speed should it be played?

**3 TV AND RADIO**

Dirk Benedict played Templeton Peck, also known as Face, in which 1980s TV show?

**4 SPORT AND LEISURE**

In golf, by what name is a score of two under par on a single hole known?

**5 GEOGRAPHY**

One country joined the UN in 1949. Which was it?

**6 SCIENCE AND NATURE**

Which element is the first in the periodic table?

**7 ART**

Which 19th-century artist cut off part of his ear after a quarrel with Gauguin?

**8 CELEBRITIES**

Which actress, who plays Betty Suarez in the US TV show *Ugly Betty*, had her smile insured for $10 million in 2007?

**9 WORDS**

What does to 'objure' mean?
- a) to make unclear
- b) to put on oath
- c) to put at right angles

**10 POT LUCK**

Which star is known as the Dog Star?

ANSWERS ON PAGE 273

# QUIZ 115

**1  MOVIES**
Which 1992 Clint Eastwood movie takes place in a town called Big Whiskey?

**2  MUSIC**
Which country does jazz singer Silje Nergaard come from?

**3  TV AND RADIO**
What is the name of the BBC 2 comedy pop quiz hosted by Mark Lamarr from 1996 to 2005 and subsequently by Simon Amstell?

**4  SPORT AND LEISURE**
In which sport do men and women compete every two years for, respectively, the Bermuda Bowl and the Venice Cup?

**5  HISTORY**
In 1961 who became the first man in space?

**6  GEOGRAPHY**
What is the name of the world's largest lake?

**7  LITERATURE**
What is the title of the Richard Adams novel about a colony of rabbits led by Hazel?

**8  SCIENCE AND NATURE**
*Malus pumila* is the Latin name of which common fruit?

**9  WORDS**
'Polyandry' means the practice of having more than one what?
        a) wife
        b) husband
        c) child

**10  POT LUCK**
On which date each year does St Andrew's day fall?

ANSWERS ON PAGE 274

# QUIZ 116

**1  MOVIES**
In which 1970s movie does Richard Burton use psychic powers to cause a plane crash?

**2  MUSIC**
'Ebeneezer Goode' was a 1990s Number One for which band?

**3  TV AND RADIO**
Who wrote the *Talking Heads* series of TV monologues?

**4  SPORT AND LEISURE**
*Raging Bull* is the life story of which boxer?

**5  HISTORY**
Which US president started the 'New Deal' programme in 1933?

**6  SCIENCE AND NATURE**
What number is signified by the Roman numerals XC?

**7  LITERATURE**
Which author wrote *Tales of the City* and its San Francisco-based sequels?

**8  CELEBRITIES**
The supermodel Heidi Klum had a son by which singer?

**9  WORDS**
What is a 'tatterdemalion'?
        a) a weed
        b) a scruffy person
        c) a type of moth

**10  POT LUCK**
The Indian god Ganesha is depicted with the head of which animal?

ANSWERS ON PAGE 274

# QUIZ 117

**1 MOVIES**
Jennifer Connelly won a Best Supporting Actress Oscar for which 2001 movie?

**2 MUSIC**
Which band's first three singles, 'Swing the Mood', 'That's What I Like' and 'Let's Party' were all Number One hits in 1989?

**3 TV AND RADIO**
Angela Channing, Chase Gioberti and Lance Cumson were all characters in a TV soap set in the fictional Tuscany Valley in California. What was the name of the soap?

**4 SPORT AND LEISURE**
Which fast bowler who played for Sussex and Worcestershire led Pakistan to victory in the 1992 cricket World Cup?

**5 HISTORY**
Who was the last Tudor monarch?

**6 GEOGRAPHY**
Helsinki is the capital city of which country?

**7 LITERATURE**
Which horror writer established the Cthulhu Mythos of elder gods?

**8 SCIENCE AND NATURE**
Which is the second planet from the Sun?

**9 WORDS**
'Homiletics' is the art of what?
  a) poetry
  b) decoration
  c) preaching

**10 POT LUCK**
What is the highest British naval rank?

ANSWERS ON PAGE 274

# QUIZ 118

**1 MOVIES**
Which country did Peter Jackson use as Middle Earth in the *Lord of the Rings* trilogy?

**2 MUSIC**
'We're Going to Ibiza!' was a Number One for which band in September 1999?

**3 TV AND RADIO**
Who was the keyboard player in rock group Yes?

**4 SPORT AND LEISURE**
Which British motorcyclist won the 500cc world championship in 1976 and 1977?

**5 HISTORY**
Which calendar was adopted in Britain in 1752?

**6 SCIENCE AND NATURE**
Where in India was the disastrous 1984 Union Carbide toxic gas leak?

**7 LITERATURE**
Which British writer won the Nobel Prize for literature in 2005?

**8 CELEBRITIES**
Who is the famous film star father of Jamie Lee Curtis?

**9 WORDS**
What is a 'sarsen'?
        a) a breed of horse
        b) a nomadic warrior
        c) a stone

**10 POT LUCK**
How is Queen Boudicca reputed to have died?

ANSWERS ON PAGE 274

# QUIZ 119

**1  MOVIES**
Kint, Hockney, McManus, Fenster and Keaton are the names of the five central characters in which 1990s movie?

**2  MUSIC**
What was the title of the song sung by Celine Dion in the film *Titanic*?

**3  TV AND RADIO**
John Barron played which character in *The Fall and Rise of Reginald Perrin*?

**4  SPORT AND LEISURE**
Which US baseball player was nicknamed 'Joltin' Joe'?

**5  HISTORY**
In which war were the battles of Shiloh, Chancellorsville and Chattanooga?

**6  GEOGRAPHY**
Calgary and Edmonton are in which Canadian province?

**7  LITERATURE**
Which novel begins with the words 'It was the best of times, it was the worst of times'?

**8  SCIENCE AND NATURE**
Who is principally famous for developing the bouncing bomb used to breach dams in World War II?

**9  WORDS**
Who rules in a 'plutocracy'?
        a) scientists
        b) the rich
        c) priests

**10  POT LUCK**
In which year was the United Nations founded?

ANSWERS ON PAGE 274

# QUIZ 120

**1 MOVIES**
Arnold Schwarzenegger starred with Max von Sydow in which 1980s fantasy movie?

**2 MUSIC**
Which jazz trumpeter and singer was nicknamed 'Satchmo'?

**3 TV AND RADIO**
Which Warrior Princess did Lucy Lawless play on TV?

**4 SPORT AND LEISURE**
For which country did footballer Mark Lawrenson win 39 international caps?

**5 GEOGRAPHY**
Nottingham stands on which river?

**6 SCIENCE AND NATURE**
Which natural gemstone is usually red?

**7 LITERATURE**
What was former SAS soldier Andy McNab's first autobiographical book called?

**8 CELEBRITIES**
Sophie Anderton has been romantically linked with which former Manchester United goalkeeper?

**9 WORDS**
What does 'jejune' mean?
        a) cowardly
        b) naive
        c) attractive

**10 POT LUCK**
According to the song, what did my true love give to me on the fifth day of Christmas?

ANSWERS ON PAGE 274

# QUIZ 121

**1 MOVIES**
Who played Larry Talbot, the eponymous monster in the 1941 horror movie *The Wolf Man*?

**2 MUSIC**
Who composed the oratorios *Saul*, *Israel in Egypt* and *The Messiah*?

**3 TV AND RADIO**
Which titular super heroine was played by Lynda Carter in a US TV show of the 1970s?

**4 SPORT AND LEISURE**
In which country was golfer Gary Player born?

**5 HISTORY**
Who was elected president of South Africa in 1994?

**6 SCIENCE AND NATURE**
Hydrogen was discovered in 1766 by which English chemist?

**7 LITERATURE**
What is the name of the wise old bear in Kipling's *The Jungle Book*?

**8 CELEBRITIES**
Christina Aguilera, Lil'Kim, Mya and Pink had a Number One hit with 'Lady Marmalade' from the soundtrack of which film?

**9 WORDS**
A 'bucolic' scene would be set where?
 - a) the countryside
 - b) by the sea
 - c) in a city

**10 POT LUCK**
Who was the first European to visit the Australian inlet called Botany Bay?

ANSWERS ON PAGE 275

# QUIZ 122

**1 MOVIES**
In which controversial 1970s Sam Peckinpah movie did Susan George star?

**2 MUSIC**
'Mad World' and 'Everybody Wants to Rule the World' were hits for which band in the 1980s?

**3 TV AND RADIO**
Patrick Macnee played which character in *The Avengers* and *The New Avengers*?

**4 SPORT AND LEISURE**
In which sport are both the Orange Bowl and the Rose Bowl competed for?

**5 HISTORY**
Which king commissioned the Domesday Book?

**6 SCIENCE AND NATURE**
Where in the body would you find the 'Malphigian layer'?

**7 LITERATURE**
Detective Inspector John Rebus features in a series of novels by which crime writer?

**8 CELEBRITIES**
Which US rapper's real name is Calvin Broadus?

**9 WORDS**
If someone is 'verecund', what are they?
- a) fertile
- b) truthful
- c) modest

**10 POT LUCK**
Which type of raffle is named after the Italian word meaning 'to tumble'?

ANSWERS ON PAGE 275

# QUIZ 123

**1   MOVIES**
Which Tod Browning horror movie of the 1930s scandalized audiences by using genuinely disabled actors?

**2   MUSIC**
Which musician, who celebrated his 60th birthday in 2007, was born in Pinner as Reginald Kenneth Dwight?

**3   TV AND RADIO**
Which famous former Mayor of Cincinnati hosted Miss World in 2000?

**4   SPORT AND LEISURE**
The pitcher's plate, also known as the rubber, is a feature in which sport?

**5   HISTORY**
In which year was the Russian Revolution?

**6   SCIENCE AND NATURE**
Wolfram is a former name for which element?

**7   LITERATURE**
In Lionel Shriver's Orange Prize-winning novel, who do 'we need to talk about'?

**8   CELEBRITIES**
Matt Damon and Heath Ledger starred in which 2005 Terry Gilliam film?

**9   WORDS**
What is a 'pirogue'?
        a) a dance
        b) a robber
        c) a canoe

**10   POT LUCK**
*Head* was a weird 1960s movie starring which early boy band?

ANSWERS ON PAGE 275

# QUIZ 124

**1 MOVIES**

*American Pie* star Tara Reid starred with Summer Phoenix in which 1998 Jonathan Kahn film?

**2 MUSIC**

Who played didgeridoo on the 1982 single 'The Dreaming' by Kate Bush?

**3 TV AND RADIO**

In *Porridge*, who played Godber?

**4 SPORT AND LEISURE**

In boxing, which weight comes between flyweight and featherweight?

**5 HISTORY**

Which battle was fought near Stirling on 21 June 1314?

**6 SCIENCE AND NATURE**

Which North African and Middle Eastern plant curls into a ball during droughts?

**7 LITERATURE**

Who wrote the Barsetshire novels?

**8 CELEBRITIES**

Ozzy, Sharon, Jack and Kelly are the most high-profile members of which famous family?

**9 WORDS**

A 'haruspex' would practise divination using what?
  a) animal entrails
  b) bird flight
  c) tarot cards

**10 POT LUCK**

Which two tools combined to make the emblem of the former USSR?

ANSWERS ON PAGE 275

# QUIZ 125

**1 MOVIES**
Which character is played by the singer Alanis Morisette in Kevin Smith's movie *Dogma*?

**2 MUSIC**
Which jazz saxophonist was nicknamed 'Bird'?

**3 TV AND RADIO**
Ed Bishop played Commander Straker in which Gerry Anderson TV series of the 1970s?

**4 SPORT AND LEISURE**
In which year did Roger Bannister run the first sub-four-minute mile?

**5 HISTORY**
Who was the second US president?

**6 GEOGRAPHY**
Harare is the capital city of which country?

**7 LITERATURE**
Who wrote *A Clockwork Orange*?

**8 SCIENCE AND NATURE**
What does a pH value of less than 7 indicate: acidity or alkalinity?

**9 WORDS**
'Pachyderms' have what, specifically?
- a) thick skin
- b) long noses
- c) sharp tusks

**10 POT LUCK**
Which word meaning traitor or collaborator comes from the name of the man who headed Norway's government from 1942?

ANSWERS ON PAGE 275

# QUIZ 126

**1 MOVIES**
Which Terry Gilliam movie starred both Michael Palin and Robert De Niro?

**2 MUSIC**
What was the title of the first UK Number One by Britney Spears?

**3 TV AND RADIO**
Richie Benaud is most famous for commentating on which sport?

**4 SPORT AND LEISURE**
Which British driver won the Formula 1 world championship in 1976?

**5 HISTORY**
What was the name of the ship built for the Norwegian explorer Fridtjof Nansen, in which he hoped to become frozen in sea ice and hence drift to the North Pole?

**6 GEOGRAPHY**
Calabria, Umbria and Lombardia are regions of which country?

**7 LITERATURE**
Who wrote *The Hitchhiker's Guide to the Galaxy*?

**8 SCIENCE AND NATURE**
What is the condition 'hypermetropia' better known as?

**9 WORDS**
Which dessert has a name that comes from a French phrase meaning 'white food'?
  - a) tiramisu
  - b) trifle
  - c) blancmange

**10 POT LUCK**
Born Amy Lyon, this woman became Nelson's mistress and bore him a daughter called Horatia. Under what name is she better known?

ANSWERS ON PAGE 275

# QUIZ 127

**1 MOVIES**
In which Kevin Spacey movie did Mena Suvari star?

**2 MUSIC**
More famous as part of a duo, who had a solo UK Number One in 1975 with 'I Only Have Eyes for You'?

**3 TV AND RADIO**
Who read *The Old Man of Lochnagar* on *Jackanory* in 1984?

**4 SPORT AND LEISURE**
Which English Rugby Union captain was sacked in 1995 for calling the sport's administrators 'old farts'?

**5 HISTORY**
Who was the last woman to receive the death penalty in Britain?

**6 SCIENCE AND NATURE**
Pack, shelf, sea, black and pancake are all kinds of what?

**7 ART**
Which artist pioneered 'action painting' before his death in a car crash in 1956?

**8 CELEBRITIES**
In which movie did Helena Bonham Carter star with Meat Loaf?

**9 WORDS**
In which activity would you use a 'punty'?
- a) blowing glass
- b) baking pies
- c) shooting pigeons

**10 POT LUCK**
What kind of geographical feature are the South Sandwich, Tonga, Yap, Mariana and Kermadec?

ANSWERS ON PAGE 276

# QUIZ 128

**1  MOVIES**
In which movie adaptation of a Charles Frazier novel did Renée Zellweger star?

**2  MUSIC**
'Lay Your Love on Me' and 'Some Girls' were chart hits for which 1970s band?

**3  TV AND RADIO**
In which US sitcom did Pam Dawber star with Robin Williams?

**4  SPORT AND LEISURE**
How many players are there in a basketball team?

**5  GEOGRAPHY**
What was Myanmar known as before 1989?

**6  SCIENCE AND NATURE**
Which animal spreads dengue fever?

**7  ART**
By what name is the painting *La Gioconda* better known?

**8  CELEBRITIES**
Who played Victor Meldrew's wife Margaret in *One Foot in the Grave*?

**9  WORDS**
What sort of animal is a 'herdwick'?
>    a) a cow
>    b) a sheep
>    c) an elephant

**10  POT LUCK**
In the commonly used simile, which vegetable might you be as cool as?

ANSWERS ON PAGE 276

# QUIZ 129

**1  MOVIES**
The Hitchcock movie *Strangers on a Train* and the 1999 film *The Talented Mr Ripley* are based on books by which crime writer?

**2  MUSIC**
In which Beatles song would you meet Father McKenzie?

**3  TV AND RADIO**
Who played Gary in *Men Behaving Badly*?

**4  SPORT AND LEISURE**
Which black US athlete won four gold medals in the 1936 Berlin Olympics?

**5  HISTORY**
Which English king succeeded Richard I, ruling from 1199 to 1216?

**6  GEOGRAPHY**
On which Scottish island would you find Tobermory?

**7  LITERATURE**
What was the title of Margaret Mitchell's only novel?

**8  SCIENCE AND NATURE**
In which organ of the body are the aortic valve and the tricuspid valve?

**9  WORDS**
What is 'kismet'?
> a) a style of music
> b) destiny
> c) a Turkish biscuit

**10  POT LUCK**
What appears in the top of the pyramid on the reverse side of a US dollar bill?

ANSWERS ON PAGE 276

# QUIZ 130

**1 MOVIES**

Which 1986 movie featured 'Be Kind to my Mistakes' by Kate Bush?

**2 MUSIC**

According to Paul Hardcastle's 1985 hit, what was the average age of a combat soldier in Vietnam?

**3 TV AND RADIO**

In which landmark BBC thriller did Joanne Whalley play murder victim Emma Craven?

**4 SPORT AND LEISURE**

Which former manager of the Scottish national football team died on 1 February 2004?

**5 HISTORY**

Which venerable Anglo-Saxon scholar wrote *The Ecclesiastical History of the English People* in the 8th century?

**6 SCIENCE AND NATURE**

What kind of animal is an 'ocelot'?

**7 LITERATURE**

In which Dickens novel is Mr Micawber a character?

**8 CELEBRITIES**

Which Hollywood star has Kelly Preston twice married?

**9 WORDS**

What is a 'moue'?
- a) a pout
- b) a chocolate sauce
- c) a jump in ballet

**10 POT LUCK**

In the Bible, who was Ahab's infamous wife?

ANSWERS ON PAGE 276

# QUIZ 131

**1 MOVIES**

Which English actor played the title role in Steven Soderbergh's movie *The Limey*?

**2 MUSIC**

'Drones', 'chanter' and 'blowstick' are part of which musical instrument?

**3 TV AND RADIO**

Stan, Kyle, Kenny and Cartman feature in which animated TV show?

**4 SPORT AND LEISURE**

'La Grande Boucle' is an alternative name for which cycle race?

**5 GEOGRAPHY**

Yell and Unst belong to which island group?

**6 SCIENCE AND NATURE**

Which animals would you find in an apiary?

**7 LITERATURE**

Who wrote *Brideshead Revisited*?

**8 CELEBRITIES**

In which country was Elisha Cuthbert, star of *The Girl Next Door* and the cult TV series *24*, born?

**9 WORDS**

What is a 'fiacre'?
- a) a disaster
- b) a carriage
- c) an inferno

**10 POT LUCK**

A 'pony' is slang for how much money?

ANSWERS ON PAGE 276

# QUIZ 132

**1  MOVIES**
Who played the robot Gigolo Joe in Steven Spielberg's *A.I. Artificial Intelligence*?

**2  MUSIC**
Who had a Top Ten hit with 'Groove is in the Heart' in 1990?

**3  TV AND RADIO**
Who has been the principal presenter of Channel 4 News since 1989?

**4  SPORT AND LEISURE**
Which US athlete was men's singles champion at Wimbledon in 1974 and 1982?

**5  HISTORY**
Who was Queen Elizabeth II's paternal grandfather?

**6  GEOGRAPHY**
Of which country is Jakarta the capital?

**7  LITERATURE**
Whose published diaries record, among many other things, the Great Fire of London?

**8  SCIENCE AND NATURE**
Which scientist famously voyaged on a ship called *The Beagle*?

**9  WORDS**
In Australia, a 'brumby' is a wild what?
  a) rabbit
  b) horse
  c) dog

**10  POT LUCK**
What does UNESCO stand for?

ANSWERS ON PAGE 276

# QUIZ 133

**1 MOVIES**

Who directed the 1973 movie *Mean Streets*?

**2 MUSIC**

Which clarinettist took 'Stranger on the Shore' into the UK Top Ten in 1961?

**3 TV AND RADIO**

Which member of the BBC's *The Royle Family* was played by Caroline Aherne?

**4 SPORT AND LEISURE**

Which British athlete won a gold medal for the men's 800m event in the 1980 Olympics?

**5 HISTORY**

Which historical character had a horse called Bucephalus?

**6 SCIENCE AND NATURE**

Which Greek mathematician's theorem is concerned with the sides of a right-angled triangle?

**7 LITERATURE**

Who wrote *Uncle Tom's Cabin*?

**8 CELEBRITIES**

Which actor played a hobbit in *The Lord of the Rings* and Charlie Pace in TV's *Lost*?

**9 WORDS**

What sort of animal is described as 'vulpine'?
- a) a vulture
- b) a wolf
- c) a fox

**10 POT LUCK**

Which 1960s pop group took their name from a turning on Paternoster Row and Ave Maria Lane in London?

ANSWERS ON PAGE 277

# QUIZ 134

**1 MOVIES**
In which Bond movie did Ursula Andress play Honey Ryder?

**2 MUSIC**
Of which pop group was Errol Brown the lead singer?

**3 TV AND RADIO**
In which 1980s sitcom did Richard Briers play Martin Bryce?

**4 SPORT AND LEISURE**
Which South African-born athlete controversially clashed with Mary Decker-Slaney in the 3,000m at the 1984 Olympics?

**5 GEOGRAPHY**
Of which country is Ljubljana the capital?

**6 SCIENCE AND NATURE**
Potassium nitrate, charcoal and sulphur make up which explosive compound?

**7 LITERATURE**
Which English dramatist wrote *Tamburlaine the Great* and *The Tragical History of Dr Faustus*?

**8 CELEBRITIES**
Kate Hudson has a famous mother. Who is she?

**9 WORDS**
To 'sypher' is to what?
- a) overlap planks
- b) pump water
- c) tap phones

**10 POT LUCK**
The Frenchman Auguste Bartholdi designed which New York landmark, unveiled in 1886?

ANSWERS ON PAGE 277

# QUIZ 135

**1 MOVIES**

Who directed the first two *Terminator* movies before passing on the third?

**2 MUSIC**

How many symphonies did Beethoven complete in his lifetime?

**3 TV AND RADIO**

Which character did Antonio Fargas play in the TV show *Starsky and Hutch*?

**4 SPORT AND LEISURE**

Which Mozambique-born footballer had a distinguished career with the Portuguese side Benfica and was the top goal-scorer in the 1966 World Cup?

**5 HISTORY**

Which Greek king fled his country in 1967 after a military coup?

**6 GEOGRAPHY**

The Pyrenees mountains lie between which two countries?

**7 LITERATURE**

Who wrote *Chocolat*, *Blackberry Wine* and *Five Quarters of the Orange*?

**8 SCIENCE AND NATURE**

Which type of reptile gained its name from the Greek words for 'terrible lizard'?

**9 WORDS**

What is a 'yapok'?
> a) a diamond-studded veil
> b) a balsawood boat
> c) an opossum

**10 POT LUCK**

Of where, specifically, was Sweeney Todd the Demon Barber?

ANSWERS ON PAGE 277

# QUIZ 136

**1 MOVIES**
Who played the monster in Kenneth Branagh's 1994 film version of *Frankenstein*?

**2 MUSIC**
'I Thought It Was You' and 'Rockit' were UK hits for which jazz legend?

**3 TV AND RADIO**
Craig Sterling, Richard Barrett and Sharron Macready made up which 1960s TV team of agents?

**4 SPORT AND LEISURE**
Which boxer beat Alan Minter in 1980 to become the undisputed world middleweight champion?

**5 HISTORY**
Christopher Columbus commanded three ships on his first voyage to the New World. The *Niña*, the *Pinta* and which other?

**6 SCIENCE AND NATURE**
Charles Babbage's difference engine and analytical engine were 19th-century equivalents of which device?

**7 LITERATURE**
Sharon Stone starred in which 1990 sci-fi movie based on the Philip K Dick story *We Can Remember It for You Wholesale*?

**8 CELEBRITIES**
What is Brad Pitt's real first name?

**9 WORDS**
Charles Napier's conquest of which Asian city was supposedly signalled by the one-word dispatch 'Peccavi' – Latin for 'I have sinned'?

**10 POT LUCK**
In which institution is the Lutine bell heard?

ANSWERS ON PAGE 277

# QUIZ 137

**1 MOVIES**

'On The Air. Unaware.' This was the poster tag-line for which movie starring Jim Carrey and Laura Linney?

**2 MUSIC**

'Love Will Keep Us Together' was a hit for which oddly-named duo?

**3 TV AND RADIO**

Apart from Dick York, which actor played Darrin opposite Elizabeth Montgomery in the TV show *Bewitched*?

**4 SPORT AND LEISURE**

Who is the youngest golfer to have won the US Masters?

**5 HISTORY**

Which four letters were inscribed on the standards of ancient Rome?

**6 SCIENCE AND NATURE**

Io, Europa, Ganymede and Callisto are moons of which planet?

**7 LITERATURE**

Who wrote the *Horatio Hornblower* stories?

**8 CELEBRITIES**

Asia Argento starred with Vin Diesel in which 2002 extreme sports answer to the Bond movies?

**9 WORDS**

A 'cokuloris' is used in which branch of the arts?
- a) music
- b) film
- c) sculpture

**10 POT LUCK**

The Roman name for the River Severn is the same name as one of the original Charlie's Angels. What is it?

ANSWERS ON PAGE 277

139

# QUIZ 138

**1  MOVIES**
Barbara Stanwyck played opposite Fred MacMurray in which classic 1944 film noir?

**2  MUSIC**
Which Scottish band had hits with 'Real Gone Kid', 'Wages Day' and 'Dignity'?

**3  TV AND RADIO**
Who played Tony Soprano in Channel 4's *The Sopranos*?

**4  SPORT AND LEISURE**
Edson Arantes do Nascimento is the real name of which famously nicknamed footballer?

**5  HISTORY**
Of which country was Paul Keating the prime minister from 1991 to 1996?

**6  GEOGRAPHY**
In which country is the Sir Seretse Khama Airport?

**7  LITERATURE**
Which Brontë sister wrote *Jane Eyre*?

**8  SCIENCE AND NATURE**
Which type of particle has a name that means 'cannot be cut'?

**9  WORDS**
What do you do to something when you 'exacerbate' it?
- a) make it bigger
- b) make it worse
- c) make it taller

**10  POT LUCK**
Which band is fronted by Thom Yorke?

ANSWERS ON PAGE 277

# QUIZ 139

**1 MOVIES**

To whom were Hollywood films often credited when the actual director wished to disassociate him or herself from the movie?

**2 MUSIC**

Jan Hammer had a 1987 Top Ten hit with 'Crockett's Theme', taken from which TV series?

**3 TV AND RADIO**

Which character did Tamzin Outhwaite play in *EastEnders*?

**4 SPORT AND LEISURE**

Which Southampton FC player, who retired in 2002, was affectionately known as 'Le God'?

**5 HISTORY**

Which 18th-century French philosopher wrote *The Social Contract*?

**6 SCIENCE AND NATURE**

In mathematics, the letter 'i' represents the square root of which number?

**7 LITERATURE**

*The Day of the Triffids*, *The Midwich Cuckoos* and *The Kraken Wakes* are books by which British writer?

**8 CELEBRITIES**

Who won Best Actress Oscars for both *The Silence of the Lambs* and *The Accused*?

**9 WORDS**

What is an 'ovolo'?

      a) an extinct bird
      b) a woodwind instrument
      c) a curved architectural moulding

**10 POT LUCK**

Which calendar month was known by the Saxons as 'blood month' or 'wind month'?

ANSWERS ON PAGE 278

# QUIZ 140

**1  MOVIES**
What was Disney's first feature-length animated film?

**2  MUSIC**
'Woke Up This Morning' by Alabama 3 was used as the theme music to which TV show?

**3  TV AND RADIO**
Which 1970s Norwich-based TV programme introduced itself as 'the Quiz of the Week' each week?

**4  SPORT AND LEISURE**
Which Canadian snooker player, who died in 2003, was renowned for drinking six pints of lager before a match and then one pint per frame to calm his nerves?

**5  HISTORY**
Brian Mulroney, Kim Campbell and Jean Chrétien were successive prime ministers of which country?

**6  SCIENCE AND NATURE**
What is the cube root of 125?

**7  ART**
Which Norwegian artist is famous for his 1893 painting *The Scream*?

**8  CELEBRITIES**
What is the real name of model and media personality Jordan?

**9  WORDS**
If something is 'numinous', what is it?
> a) brightly-lit
> b) plentiful
> c) divine

**10  POT LUCK**
In the Trooping of the Colour, what is the 'Colour'?

ANSWERS ON PAGE 278

# QUIZ 141

**1 MOVIES**

Which classical actor played the part of Crassus in Stanley Kubrick's *Spartacus*?

**2 MUSIC**

With which band was Cerys Matthews the lead singer before embarking on a solo career?

**3 TV AND RADIO**

Paul Gross played mountie Constable Benton Fraser in which 1990s TV series?

**4 SPORT AND LEISURE**

For which English football club did Dixie Dean score 349 goals in 399 games?

**5 HISTORY**

Mohandas Gandhi was also known by a title meaning 'great' or 'high soul' in Sanskrit. What was that title?

**6 GEOGRAPHY**

Of which US state is Providence the capital?

**7 LITERATURE**

Who wrote *The Tale of Peter Rabbit* and many other children's stories?

**8 SCIENCE AND NATURE**

What sort of device was patented by Richard Jordan Gatling in 1862?

**9 WORDS**

What are you if you are 'parsimonious'?
- a) religious
- b) good in the kitchen
- c) frugal

**10 POT LUCK**

In which city would you find the Sears Tower?

ANSWERS ON PAGE 278

# QUIZ 142

**1  MOVIES**
Tilda Swinton starred in *Orlando*, a 1992 movie version of whose novel?

**2  MUSIC**
Which French composer wrote *Carnival of the Animals*?

**3  TV AND RADIO**
Which foodstuff was the subject of a BBC *Panorama* programme, narrated by Richard Dimbleby, on 1 April 1957 that purported to show the crop being harvested in Switzerland?

**4  SPORT AND LEISURE**
Which US tennis player turned professional on 5 March 1990 at the age of 13?

**5  HISTORY**
Who ruled Britain from 1702 to 1714?

**6  SCIENCE AND NATURE**
Opium can be extracted from the seeds of which plant?

**7  LITERATURE**
Meryl Streep starred with Clint Eastwood in a movie adaptation of which bestselling Robert James Waller novel?

**8  CELEBRITIES**
Which rapper starred in the mutant shark movie *Deep Blue Sea* and the 2002 remake of *Rollerball*?

**9  WORDS**
What is 'cupidity'?
  a) covetousness
  b) an excessive affection
  c) ability at archery

**10  POT LUCK**
What is a kirby grip designed to hold?

ANSWERS ON PAGE 278

# QUIZ 143

**1 MOVIES**

In which Jane Campion crime movie did Meg Ryan star with Mark Ruffalo?

**2 MUSIC**

In which country was Tiri Te Kanawa born?

**3 TV AND RADIO**

In which 1980s BBC comedy series did Adrian Edmondson play Vyvyan?

**4 SPORT AND LEISURE**

Which boxer's life story was depicted in the film *The Hurricane*?

**5 GEOGRAPHY**

What was the name of the tanker which spilled tens of thousands of gallons of oil off Shetland in 1993?

**6 SCIENCE AND NATURE**

In which country is the active volcano Laki?

**7 LITERATURE**

By which author are the novels *Men Like Gods* and *The History of Mr Polly*?

**8 CELEBRITIES**

Which character does Kate Ford play in *Coronation Street*?

**9 WORDS**

'Taphephobia' is a fear of being what?
- a) stabbed
- b) hit
- c) buried alive

**10 POT LUCK**

If something is described as 'infra dig', what is it beneath?

ANSWERS ON PAGE 278

# QUIZ 144

**1 MOVIES**
Which 1979 film was loosely based upon Joseph Conrad's 1899 novella *Heart of Darkness*?

**2 MUSIC**
Which music producer created the famous 'Wall of Sound'?

**3 TV AND RADIO**
Angela Rippon, Noel Edmonds and Jeremy Clarkson have all presented which BBC motoring programme?

**4 SPORT AND LEISURE**
What is the nickname of US basketball player Earvin Johnson?

**5 HISTORY**
Which famous English explorer was beheaded in Whitehall in 1618?

**6 GEOGRAPHY**
What is the name of the region of south-west Asia that lies between the Tigris and the Euphrates rivers?

**7 LITERATURE**
Who wrote the novels *The Rainbow* and *Women in Love*?

**8 SCIENCE AND NATURE**
What is 'algophobia' a fear of?

**9 WORDS**
What does 'desuetude' mean?
- a) sadness
- b) disuse
- c) loneliness

**10 POT LUCK**
Who has released albums entitled *Frank's Wild Years*, *Swordfishtrombones* and *Heartattack and Vine*?

ANSWERS ON PAGE 278

# QUIZ 145

**1  MOVIES**
Which was the first *Carry On* film?

**2  MUSIC**
Which singer had hits in the 1980s with 'New Song' and 'What is Love'?

**3  TV AND RADIO**
Who played Margery Allingham's detective character Campion on TV?

**4  SPORT AND LEISURE**
In which Olympics did Florence Griffith-Joyner win three gold medals and a silver?

**5  HISTORY**
Who was the US president for most of World War II?

**6  SCIENCE AND NATURE**
Which alloy was formerly made principally of lead and tin, and now mainly of tin with a little copper, antimony or bismuth?

**7  LITERATURE**
In which Jules Verne novel is Phileas Fogg the main character?

**8  CELEBRITIES**
In which 2001 movie did Eva Mendes play Denzel Washington's girlfriend?

**9  WORDS**
What creatures might be described as 'fringilline'?
- a) finches
- b) eagles
- c) albatrosses

**10  POT LUCK**
What is the name of the Premium Bonds random number generating machine?

ANSWERS ON PAGE 279

# QUIZ 146

**1  MOVIES**

Sean Connery and *Sopranos* star Lorraine Bracco appeared in which jungle-based movie of 1992?

**2  MUSIC**

'Wishing I Was Lucky' and 'Sweet Little Mystery' were the first two Top Ten UK hits for which band?

**3  TV AND RADIO**

Who played the eponymous New York cowboy cop McCloud in the 1970s TV series?

**4  SPORT AND LEISURE**

Which European football team play home matches at the Bernabeu?

**5  GEOGRAPHY**

What is the French stock exchange called?

**6  SCIENCE AND NATURE**

How many nautical miles are there in a degree of latitude?

**7  LITERATURE**

Which US author wrote *Slaughterhouse-Five* and *Breakfast of Champions*?

**8  CELEBRITIES**

'Ironic' and 'You Oughta Know' were hits from which album by Alanis Morissette?

**9  WORDS**

If something is 'clinquant', what is it?
- a) restricted
- b) glittering
- c) fivefold

**10  POT LUCK**

Which dance gets its name from the Czech word for half-step?

ANSWERS ON PAGE 279

# QUIZ 147

**1  MOVIES**

In *Kramer vs Kramer*, who played the estranged wife of Dustin Hoffman's character?

**2  MUSIC**

Who wrote the ballets *Swan Lake*, *The Sleeping Beauty* and *The Nutcracker*?

**3  TV AND RADIO**

In the TV show *Dempsey and Makepeace*, who played Dempsey?

**4  SPORT AND LEISURE**

Which jockey rode 1,138 winners over fences and was seven times National Hunt champion jockey before retiring to write crime novels?

**5  HISTORY**

Which 15th- and 16th-century Polish astronomer was greeted by outrage for suggesting that the sun was at the centre of the solar system?

**6  GEOGRAPHY**

With which other country did the Brenner Pass link Austria?

**7  LITERATURE**

Which US author wrote *Breakfast at Tiffany's* and *In Cold Blood*?

**8  SCIENCE AND NATURE**

What was the name of Earth's first artificial satellite, launched by the USSR in October 1957?

**9  WORDS**

What does a 'hygrometer' measure?
- a) height
- b) heat
- c) humidity

**10  POT LUCK**

Grenadine is a syrup made from the juice of which fruit?

ANSWERS ON PAGE 279

# QUIZ 148

**1 MOVIES**
Who starred as porn baron Larry Flynt in Milos Forman's 1996 movie *The People vs Larry Flynt*?

**2 MUSIC**
'Every Loser Wins' and 'Heartbeat' were UK hit singles for which actor?

**3 TV AND RADIO**
Who played Pug Henry in the 1980s TV mini-series *The Winds of War*?

**4 SPORT AND LEISURE**
Who owned Sun Chariot, the racehorse that won the fillies' Triple Crown in 1942?

**5 HISTORY**
In 1893, which country became the first to give women the right to vote?

**6 SCIENCE AND NATURE**
Which vitamin is ascorbic acid?

**7 LITERATURE**
Which French author wrote *Candide*?

**8 CELEBRITIES**
Jude Law, Gwyneth Paltrow and Angelina Jolie starred in which computer-generated 2004 movie?

**9 WORDS**
'Pyogenesis' is the creation of what?
- a) fire
- b) hair
- c) pus

**10 POT LUCK**
Which day is celebrated on the first Sunday after the Paschal full moon?

ANSWERS ON PAGE 279

# QUIZ 149

**1 MOVIES**
Who plays the luckless cabbie commandeered by Tom Cruise's hitman in *Collateral*?

**2 MUSIC**
Who had a chart hit in 1961 with 'Let's Twist Again'?

**3 TV AND RADIO**
Who won a BAFTA for her portrayal of Connie Sachs in *Tinker, Tailor, Soldier, Spy*?

**4 SPORT AND LEISURE**
'Ketaguri' is a technique in which sport?

**5 GEOGRAPHY**
In which country is Banff National Park?

**6 SCIENCE AND NATURE**
The Bessemer process is a means of producing what?

**7 ART**
In which Russian city is the State Hermitage Museum?

**8 CELEBRITIES**
In which movie update of *Dangerous Liaisons* did Sarah Michelle Gellar star?

**9 WORDS**
What is a 'jumar'?
       a) a piece of climbing equipment
       b) a pickle
       c) a wildcat

**10 POT LUCK**
Where might you find a 'bridge', a 'poop' and a 'galley'?

ANSWERS ON PAGE 279

# QUIZ 150

**1 MOVIES**
Alfred Hitchcock made three films based on Daphne du Maurier novels and short stories, including *Jamaica Inn* in 1939 and *Rebecca* in 1940. What was the third?

**2 MUSIC**
For which 1952 western movie did Dimitri Tiomkin compose the music?

**3 TV AND RADIO**
Which character did Ken Kercheval play in *Dallas*?

**4 SPORT AND LEISURE**
Which great endurance motor race was first held in 1923?

**5 HISTORY**
Long, Short, Addled, Merciless, Barebone's and Rump: all historical nicknames given at various times to which English institution?

**6 GEOGRAPHY**
In which country is the city of Malmö?

**7 LITERATURE**
Inspector Wexford is the creation of which British crime writer?

**8 SCIENCE AND NATURE**
How many sides are the same length in an isosceles triangle?

**9 WORDS**
'Onomatopoeia' describes the use of what type of word? One that:
> a) is unnecessary
> b) is too long
> c) sounds like what it describes

**10 POT LUCK**
Which prickly British mammal is of the genus Erinaceus?

ANSWERS ON PAGE 279

# QUIZ 151

**1 MOVIES**
Which 2004 film portrays the life of Cole Porter?

**2 MUSIC**
Whose only Top Ten hit was the 1996 Number One 'Spaceman'?

**3 TV AND RADIO**
In which radio series do the Grundys and the Aldridges feature?

**4 SPORT AND LEISURE**
In which city would you find Croke Park stadium?

**5 HISTORY**
In which year did the Spanish Civil War end?

**6 SCIENCE AND NATURE**
How is the arctic whale with a long spiral tusk better known?

**7 LITERATURE**
Which African writer won the 1999 Booker prize with his novel
*Disgrace*?

**8 CELEBRITIES**
Leslie Ash starred in which 1979 Mods versus Rockers movie?

**9 WORDS**
A 'ventouse' is a medical implement designed to assist with
what?
        a) headaches
        b) childbirth
        c) flatulence

**10 POT LUCK**
Which town did the legendary Pied Piper rid of rats?

ANSWERS ON PAGE 280

# QUIZ 152

**1 MOVIES**

Which comic actor played male model Zoolander in the movie of the same name?

**2 MUSIC**

For whom was 'Are You Being Served Sir?' a novelty Top 40 hit in 1975?

**3 TV AND RADIO**

Who shared the bill with Tracey Ullman and Lenny Henry in the 1980s TV sketch show *Three of a Kind*?

**4 SPORT AND LEISURE**

Which Romanian footballer has been called the 'Maradona of the Carpathians'?

**5 HISTORY**

How was the British financial crisis of 1720 known?

**6 SCIENCE AND NATURE**

Which French scientist developed a way to sterilize milk, etc, using a short heat treatment?

**7 LITERATURE**

Who was the British Poet Laureate from 1972 to 1984?

**8 CELEBRITIES**

In what field is Richard Rogers, Lord Rogers of Riverside, well-known?

**9 WORDS**

What is the 'distaff side'?
- a) the tail side on a coin
- b) the right side of a shield
- c) the female side of a family

**10 POT LUCK**

Which slapstick team of policemen featured in a series of silent movies?

ANSWERS ON PAGE 280

154

# QUIZ 153

**1  MOVIES**
In the *Pink Panther* movies, what actually is the 'Pink Panther'?

**2  MUSIC**
For which James Bond film did Lulu sing the theme tune?

**3  TV AND RADIO**
Which classic *Coronation Street* character was played by
Christopher Quinten?

**4  SPORT AND LEISURE**
Which British athlete won the London women's marathon in
1996?

**5  HISTORY**
Which English conflict lasted from 1455 to 1485?

**6  GEOGRAPHY**
What is the capital city of Australia?

**7  LITERATURE**
*The Autograph Man* was the second novel by which
contemporary British writer?

**8  SCIENCE AND NATURE**
The four bases of DNA are described by the letters C, G, T and
what?

**9  WORDS**
To 'susurrate' means what?
>               a) to whisper
>               b) to talk
>               c) to shout

**10  POT LUCK**
Which hero led the Argonauts in a quest for the Golden Fleece?

ANSWERS ON PAGE 280

# QUIZ 154

**1 MOVIES**
Who played Batman in *Batman Forever*?

**2 MUSIC**
'My Old Man's a Dustman' and 'Does Your Chewing Gum Lose Its Flavour' were hits for which UK skiffle star?

**3 TV AND RADIO**
Who played Chief Whip Francis Urquhart in *House of Cards* and its TV sequels?

**4 SPORT AND LEISURE**
Which distance runner was born in Northwich, Cheshire, on 17 December 1973?

**5 GEOGRAPHY**
What was the former name of the shipping forecast area FitzRoy, which was renamed in 2002?

**6 SCIENCE AND NATURE**
What is measured by a galvanometer?

**7 LITERATURE**
Lynda La Plante's *Prime Suspect* novels were televised starring Helen Mirren as who?

**8 CELEBRITIES**
In which contract killer movie of 1997 did Minnie Driver star with John Cusack?

**9 WORDS**
Where would you find an 'umbo'?
  a) on a toadstool
  b) on a sundial
  c) in an aeroplane

**10 POT LUCK**
Which institution is also known as the 'Old Lady of Threadneedle Street'?

ANSWERS ON PAGE 280

# QUIZ 155

**1 MOVIES**

Meg Ryan, Billy Crystal and Carrie Fisher appeared in which 1980s Rob Reiner movie?

**2 MUSIC**

Which group finally had a Number One hit with 'Young at Heart' when it re-entered the charts in 1993?

**3 TV AND RADIO**

Who played Dr Sam Beckett in *Quantum Leap*?

**4 SPORT AND LEISURE**

What nationality is skier Janica Kostelić?

**5 GEOGRAPHY**

In which country are the cities of Bergen and Stavanger?

**6 SCIENCE AND NATURE**

Dian Fossey is known for her research work with which animals?

**7 LITERATURE**

In which castle does Titus Groan live in a series of books by Mervyn Peake?

**8 CELEBRITIES**

Kirstie Alley played Rebecca Howe in which long-running US TV sitcom?

**9 WORDS**

To 'obnubilate' means to what?
  a) darken
  b) cripple
  c) block

**10 POT LUCK**

Which now-classic novel was the subject of an Old Bailey obscenity trial in 1960?

ANSWERS ON PAGE 280

# QUIZ 156

**1  MOVIES**
Jane Wyman and Ray Milland's 1945 movie *The Lost Weekend* was about the devastating effects of which condition?

**2  MUSIC**
What was the composer Mahler's first name?

**3  TV AND RADIO**
Around which city was the BBC detective drama *Shoestring* set?

**4  SPORT AND LEISURE**
Which British athlete, who won eleven gold Paralympic medals, announced her retirement in 2007?

**5  GEOGRAPHY**
Of which country did Hosni Mubarak become president in 1981?

**6  SCIENCE AND NATURE**
The 'strandwolf' is a species of which animal?

**7  LITERATURE**
John Yossarian and Milo Minderbender are characters in which influential 20th-century novel?

**8  CELEBRITIES**
Aishwarya Rai plays Lalita in which Bollywood adaptation of a Jane Austen novel?

**9  WORDS**
If something is 'desultory' what is it?
- a) dismissive
- b) haphazard
- c) insulting

**10  POT LUCK**
What is the more familiar name of the shape also known as a 'gammadion'?

ANSWERS ON PAGE 280

# QUIZ 157

**1 MOVIES**
Who played Butch in *Butch Cassidy and the Sundance Kid*?

**2 MUSIC**
'Superstition', 'My Cherie Amour' and 'Sir Duke' were hits for whom?

**3 TV AND RADIO**
Josette Simon played Dayna in which BBC sci-fi series of the 1970s and 1980s?

**4 SPORT AND LEISURE**
What is Maradona's first name?

**5 HISTORY**
Who was Edward VII's mother?

**6 GEOGRAPHY**
Of which US state is Santa Fe the capital?

**7 LITERATURE**
Which prominent British novelist published *Yellow Dog* in 2003?

**8 SCIENCE AND NATURE**
'Felidae' describes the family of which animals?

**9 WORDS**
What is a 'compotation'?
  a) a drinking party
  b) a fruit preserve
  c) a piece of algebra

**10 POT LUCK**
Which form of popular entertainment derives its name from the Japanese words for 'empty orchestra'?

ANSWERS ON PAGE 281

# QUIZ 158

**1 MOVIES**
Bruce Willis provided the baby's voice for which 1989 film comedy starring Kirstie Alley and John Travolta?

**2 MUSIC**
Which group had 1980s hits with 'Alive and Kicking', 'Don't You (Forget About Me)' and 'Belfast Child'?

**3 TV AND RADIO**
Who starred as Hamish Macbeth in the TV series of the same name?

**4 SPORT AND LEISURE**
Which England goalkeeper's career was ended by an eye injury sustained in 1972?

**5 GEOGRAPHY**
What is the capital city of Cuba?

**6 SCIENCE AND NATURE**
Which organ of the body does 'nephritis' affect?

**7 LITERATURE**
Who wrote *The Wind in the Willows*?

**8 CELEBRITIES**
Which Hollywood star does Cate Blanchett play in Martin Scorsese's movie *The Aviator*?

**9 WORDS**
Something 'eldritch' is what?
  a) weird
  b) made of wood
  c) more than 100 years old

**10 POT LUCK**
Which wedding anniversary is associated with crystal?

ANSWERS ON PAGE 281

# QUIZ 159

**1  MOVIES**
Charlize Theron won an Oscar in 2004 for her portrayal of a serial killer in which film?

**2  MUSIC**
Which group had hits in the 1990s with 'Common People', 'Disco 2000' and 'Help the Aged'?

**3  TV AND RADIO**
In the 1950s TV series, which title character could be found behind the throttle of the Cannonball Express?

**4  SPORT AND LEISURE**
In golf, the Ryder Cup is competed for by which two teams?

**5  HISTORY**
How many archbishops of Canterbury were there between 1645 and 1660?

**6  GEOGRAPHY**
O'Hare is the international airport for which US city?

**7  LITERATURE**
Which French author wrote *Remembrance of Things Past*?

**8  SCIENCE AND NATURE**
How is the food additive E330 better known?

**9  WORDS**
In which church service would you use a 'catafalque'?
- a) a christening
- b) a marriage
- c) a funeral

**10  POT LUCK**
What was banned in public places in Scotland in March 2006, in Northern Ireland and Wales in April 2007 and in England in July 2007?

ANSWERS ON PAGE 281

# QUIZ 160

**1 MOVIES**
Michelle Pfeiffer starred as Isabeau with Rutger Hauer and Matthew Broderick in which 1980s fantasy movie?

**2 MUSIC**
Who was the lead singer of Queen?

**3 TV AND RADIO**
What kind of animal was Flipper in the 1960s TV series of the same name?

**4 SPORT AND LEISURE**
Which Juventus and then Middlesbrough football player was known as the 'White Feather'?

**5 HISTORY**
Which saint's day is 1 March?

**6 SCIENCE AND NATURE**
In which organ of the body would you find alveoli?

**7 ART**
Which architect designed the Royal Observatory, Greenwich and St Paul's Cathedral?

**8 CELEBRITIES**
Diane Kruger stars with Nicolas Cage, Sean Bean and Harvey Keitel in which action movie?

**9 WORDS**
What is a 'whimbrel'?
> a) a stupid person
> b) a haystack
> c) a bird

**10 POT LUCK**
Which Chinese game is played with 136 or 144 tiles, including bamboo, circle and character suits?

ANSWERS ON PAGE 281

# QUIZ 161

**1 MOVIES**
Which singer played Major Marco in the 1962 film *The Manchurian Candidate*?

**2 MUSIC**
'Nights in White Satin' was a hit for which Birmingham rock quintet?

**3 TV AND RADIO**
Ulrika Jonsson started her career as a weather forecaster on which TV station?

**4 SPORT AND LEISURE**
In the US NFL, which city's team is called the 49ers?

**5 HISTORY**
Which stateswoman was prime minister of Israel from 1969 to 1974?

**6 GEOGRAPHY**
Of which country is Ulan Bator the capital?

**7 LITERATURE**
Who wrote the hit horror novels *Carrie*, *The Shining* and *Misery*?

**8 SCIENCE AND NATURE**
What, in physics, is measured using the pascal as a unit?

**9 WORDS**
What does 'discombobulate' mean?
        a) to disconcert
        b) to dishevel
        c) to disembowel

**10 POT LUCK**
Malmesbury and Stellenbosch are winemaking areas in which country?

ANSWERS ON PAGE 281

# QUIZ 162

**1 MOVIES**
Charlotte Rampling and Bo Derek starred in which 1977 post-*Jaws* ocean threat movie?

**2 MUSIC**
Which US jazz pianist started life as Ferdinand Joseph La Menthe or Lamothe?

**3 TV AND RADIO**
In *The Simpsons*, what is the name of the Mayor of Springfield?

**4 SPORT AND LEISURE**
On which continent was lacrosse invented?

**5 HISTORY**
Which 16th-century French astrologer expressed his supposed predictions in rhyming quatrains?

**6 SCIENCE AND NATURE**
Which founder of a series of prizes, including a peace prize, invented dynamite?

**7 LITERATURE**
The writer of the *Raffles* stories, E W Hornung, was the brother-in-law of which more famous author?

**8 CELEBRITIES**
Julie Gonzalo played Amber the cheerleader in which spoof sports movie of 2004?

**9 WORDS**
If something is 'postprandial', what does it follow?
        a) a meal
        b) a walk
        c) a crash

**10 POT LUCK**
Which French couturier is credited with introducing the 'little black dress'?

ANSWERS ON PAGE 281

# QUIZ 163

1 **MOVIES**
Who played Sam in *Casablanca*?

2 **MUSIC**
Which two Abba singles reached Number One in the UK charts in 1980?

3 **TV AND RADIO**
Who did Sheila Mercier play in *Emmerdale Farm*?

4 **SPORT AND LEISURE**
Who was WBO world featherweight boxing champion from 1995 to 1999?

5 **HISTORY**
During which US president's administration were California and New Mexico acquired?

6 **GEOGRAPHY**
Which continent has the largest land area?

7 **LITERATURE**
Who wrote *The Water Babies*?

8 **SCIENCE AND NATURE**
Who is credited with inventing the miner's safety lamp?

9 **WORDS**
What was a 'tidewaiter'?
        a) a now-extinct bird
        b) a fisherman's bag
        c) a customs official

10 **POT LUCK**
What was the name of one of the Egyptian gods of the dead, portrayed with the head of a jackal?

ANSWERS ON PAGE 282

# QUIZ 164

**1 MOVIES**
Which 1996 movie told the true story of piano prodigy David Helfgott?

**2 MUSIC**
With which band was Björk the singer before her solo career?

**3 TV AND RADIO**
Who played Bob Ferris in *The Likely Lads*?

**4 SPORT AND LEISURE**
Which baseball team brought shame on the sport by conspiring to lose the World Series in 1919?

**5 HISTORY**
Which country did Turkey, France, Sardinia and Britain fight in the Crimean War?

**6 SCIENCE AND NATURE**
'Rutabaga' is the US name for which vegetable?

**7 LITERATURE**
Of which crime writer was Mike Hammer the creation?

**8 CELEBRITIES**
What are celebrity favourites Annabel's, Boujis and Chinawhite?

**9 WORDS**
A 'heuristic' process does what?
- a) records time
- b) assists learning
- c) improves vision

**10 POT LUCK**
What is the name of the World Tree which supports the sky in Norse mythology?

ANSWERS ON PAGE 282

# QUIZ 165

**1 MOVIES**
In which Fellini movie did Anita Ekberg dance in the Trevi fountain in Rome?

**2 MUSIC**
Which Beethoven symphony is also known as the 'Pastoral'?

**3 TV AND RADIO**
Who played Poncherello in *CHiPS*?

**4 SPORT AND LEISURE**
Serge Blanco was a French star in which sport?

**5 HISTORY**
Who preceded Mikhail Gorbachev as president of the USSR?

**6 GEOGRAPHY**
Monte Carlo forms part of which principality?

**7 LITERATURE**
Which politician wrote a six-volume history of World War II?

**8 SCIENCE AND NATURE**
What sort of animal is a 'pipistrelle'?

**9 WORDS**
'Antediluvian' means dating from before which event?
     a) the Norman Conquest
     b) the biblical flood
     c) the dawn of time

**10 POT LUCK**
Which number month was October in the Roman calendar?

ANSWERS ON PAGE 282

# QUIZ 166

**1 MOVIES**
Judi Dench played Mistress Quickly in which Kenneth Branagh Shakespeare adaptation?

**2 MUSIC**
Which duo from *Opportunity Knocks* topped the charts with 'Welcome Home' in 1973?

**3 TV AND RADIO**
Which former choir boy presents the Radio 2 show *Good Morning Sunday*?

**4 SPORT AND LEISURE**
Which Australian cricket captain ordered his brother Trevor to bowl a pea-roller in order to beat New Zealand in 1981?

**5 HISTORY**
Charlemagne was the king of which race of people?

**6 SCIENCE AND NATURE**
The Marburg virus is also known by what colourful term?

**7 LITERATURE**
*The Long Way Round* is an account of an epic motorcycle journey by Charley Boorman and which other actor?

**8 CELEBRITIES**
Jeri Ryan plays the alien Seven of Nine, a crew member aboard which spaceship?

**9 WORDS**
In Canada, which professional might use a 'peavey'?
- a) a mountie
- b) a miner
- c) a logger

**10 POT LUCK**
In a commonly-used simile, which bird might you be as proud as?

ANSWERS ON PAGE 282

# QUIZ 167

**1 MOVIES**
What is the name of Al Pacino's 1975 movie about a bungled bank raid?

**2 MUSIC**
Eddie Rabbitt performed the theme song for which 1978 movie?

**3 TV AND RADIO**
*Sex and the City*'s Kim Cattrall played a Vulcan in which *Star Trek* movie?

**4 SPORT AND LEISURE**
How was bullfighter Manuel Benítez Pérez better known?

**5 HISTORY**
In which year did Switzerland join the United Nations?

**6 GEOGRAPHY**
By which country is Lesotho entirely enclosed?

**7 LITERATURE**
In which Shakespeare play would you find Duncan, Malcolm and Banquo?

**8 SCIENCE AND NATURE**
What name does the European Space Agency use for its rockets?

**9 WORDS**
An 'idioglossia' is what?
        a) a private language
        b) a mental disorder
        c) a rock formation

**10 POT LUCK**
Which sign of the zodiac represents an archer?

ANSWERS ON PAGE 282

# QUIZ 168

### 1 MOVIES
Who plays the First Lady's hapless bodyguard in *Guarding Tess*?

### 2 MUSIC
Peggy Lee provided the voice for a dog character in which 1955 Disney movie?

### 3 TV AND RADIO
Who played Gambit in *The New Avengers*?

### 4 SPORT AND LEISURE
Which sporting event is held at a venue on Church Road, London, SW19?

### 5 HISTORY
Which country was ruled by the Valois dynasty?

### 6 SCIENCE AND NATURE
Which drink is obtained from the arabica bean?

### 7 ART
What nationality was the 17th-century painter Velázquez?

### 8 CELEBRITIES
Janeane Garofalo appeared as 'the Bowler' in which spoof superhero movie?

### 9 WORDS
What is 'maccaboy' a type of?
- a) snuff
- b) toffee
- c) whisky

### 10 POT LUCK
Who had to capture an Arcadian stag, a Cretan bull and Cerberus?

ANSWERS ON PAGE 282

# QUIZ 169

**1 MOVIES**
Cameron Diaz provides the voice of Princess Fiona in which animated movie?

**2 MUSIC**
Who had a hit in the 1970s with 'On a Little Street in Singapore'?

**3 TV AND RADIO**
What was the name of the carved wooden bookend in the shape of a woodpecker in the TV programme *Bagpuss*?

**4 SPORT AND LEISURE**
Which English football team is nicknamed 'the Rams'?

**5 HISTORY**
Who was the Greek goddess of victory?

**6 GEOGRAPHY**
Of which country did Michelle Bachelet become president in 2007?

**7 LITERATURE**
'John Ronald Reuel' were the first names of which English author?

**8 SCIENCE AND NATURE**
In computing, how is 'Beginners'All-purpose Symbolic Instruction Code' better known?

**9 WORDS**
'Pisiform' means shaped like what?
- a) a fish
- b) a swimming pool
- c) a pea

**10 POT LUCK**
The airport for which UK city is situated in Dyce?

ANSWERS ON PAGE 283

# QUIZ 170

**1 MOVIES**
Which movie starring Nicole Kidman also stars Eric Sykes?

**2 MUSIC**
What was the name of Frankie Goes to Hollywood's lead singer?

**3 TV AND RADIO**
In which ITV quiz show did contestants try not to win Dusty Bin from Ted Rogers?

**4 SPORT AND LEISURE**
With which animals would you associate Harvey Smith?

**5 HISTORY**
In which year did Britain return Hong Kong to China?

**6 SCIENCE AND NATURE**
Which animal's name literally means 'river horse' in Greek?

**7 LITERATURE**
Who wrote *Three Men in a Boat*?

**8 CELEBRITIES**
Which musician and philanthropist's daughters are called Peaches, Fifi Trixibelle and Pixie?

**9 WORDS**
What is a 'baluster'?
   a) an architectural feature
   b) a rocky outcrop
   c) an undergarment

**10 POT LUCK**
Brian Rankin is better known as which guitarist?

ANSWERS ON PAGE 283

# QUIZ 171

**1 MOVIES**
Which famous novelist wrote the screenplay for the 1980s sci-fi film *Saturn 3*?

**2 MUSIC**
Which rapper had a UK Number One with 'Gangsta's Paradise'?

**3 TV AND RADIO**
Which late-night TV music show was hosted by Michaela Strachan and Pete Waterman?

**4 SPORT AND LEISURE**
Sam Snead was a famous player of which sport?

**5 HISTORY**
Who is credited with introducing printing to Europe in the mid-15th century?

**6 GEOGRAPHY**
In which island group are Lewis, Skye and Mull?

**7 LITERATURE**
Who wrote the novel *Dracula*?

**8 SCIENCE AND NATURE**
Which tanker disastrously ran aground off the coast of France in 1978?

**9 WORDS**
What is a 'lutz'?
- a) a skating manoeuvre
- b) an illuminated decoration
- c) a clumsy idiot

**10 POT LUCK**
*El País* is a daily newspaper in which European country?

ANSWERS ON PAGE 283

# QUIZ 172

**1 MOVIES**
Who plays Spider-Man in the films of 2002, 2004 and 2007?

**2 MUSIC**
Whose albums include *De Stijl*, *Elephant* and *White Blood Cells*?

**3 TV AND RADIO**
Which chat show host chaired the BBC's notorious Halloween prank *Ghostwatch*?

**4 SPORT AND LEISURE**
How many dominoes are there in a complete set?

**5 HISTORY**
How were Hastings, Romney, Hythe, Dover and Sandwich once collectively known?

**6 SCIENCE AND NATURE**
Which geological time period comes between the Triassic and the Cretaceous?

**7 ART**
Which Spanish artist painted *Guernica* in 1937?

**8 CELEBRITIES**
Who began his showbiz career as 'The Boy Bruce – The Mighty Atom'?

**9 WORDS**
If something is 'rutilant', what is it?
        a) glowing red
        b) rough and scaly
        c) ready to be planted

**10 POT LUCK**
Which French winemaking region does Chablis come from?

ANSWERS ON PAGE 283

# QUIZ 173

**1   MOVIES**
In which movie musical did Marlon Brando and Frank Sinatra star together?

**2   MUSIC**
Which composer wrote *Finlandia* and the *Karelia* suite?

**3   TV AND RADIO**
What was the title of the romantic TV sitcom that starred Zoë Wanamaker and Adam Faith?

**4   SPORT AND LEISURE**
What nationality is cyclist Eddy Merckx?

**5   HISTORY**
In which year was the Six Day War?

**6   GEOGRAPHY**
Khalkha is a dialect spoken in which country?

**7   LITERATURE**
Laura Hillenbrand wrote a bestselling account of the life of which horse?

**8   SCIENCE AND NATURE**
What are Pollux, Aldebaran, Rigel and Beta Centauri?

**9   WORDS**
What does 'adumbrate' mean?
   a) to outline
   b) to deny
   c) to conceal

**10   POT LUCK**
Which mythical nymph gave her name to a reflected sound?

ANSWERS ON PAGE 283

# QUIZ 174

**1  MOVIES**
*Ran* is Akira Kurosawa's movie version of which Shakespeare play?

**2  MUSIC**
Who wrote the operas *Tannhäuser* and *Tristan und Isolde*?

**3  TV AND RADIO**
Amanda Donohoe, Jimmy Smits and Corbin Bernsen all starred in which US legal TV series?

**4  SPORT AND LEISURE**
What would an 'arctophile' collect?

**5  HISTORY**
Ivan the Terrible was the first Russian ruler to adopt which title?

**6  SCIENCE AND NATURE**
Sir Alec Jeffreys is credited with the development of which forensic science technique?

**7  LITERATURE**
Which fictional Chinese villain was created by Sax Rohmer?

**8  CELEBRITIES**
Elle MacPherson starred with Hugh Grant and Sam Neill in which sultry 1994 movie?

**9  WORDS**
In the Orient, what was a 'palanquin'?
- a) a warlord
- b) a means of transport and leisure
- c) a geisha

**10  POT LUCK**
Which novel was Jane Austen writing when she died?

ANSWERS ON PAGE 283

# QUIZ 175

**1  MOVIES**
In which 1995 comic book movie adaptation did Sylvester Stallone star?

**2  MUSIC**
'Tiger Feet' and 'Oh Boy' were Number One hits for which group?

**3  TV AND RADIO**
Alex Kingston, William H Macy and George Clooney have all starred in which US medical TV drama?

**4  SPORT AND LEISURE**
What kind of sporting animal was Mick the Miller?

**5  HISTORY**
Who won the Nobel Peace Prize in 1979?

**6  GEOGRAPHY**
Djibouti has borders with Somalia, Eritrea and which other country?

**7  LITERATURE**
Who wrote the novels *Disclosure* and *Timeline*?

**8  SCIENCE AND NATURE**
The 'islets of Langerhans' are situated in which organ of the body?

**9  WORDS**
What is a 'quincunx'?
       a) a hand of cards
       b) a big cat
       c) an arrangement of five objects

**10  POT LUCK**
Who was the first Inquisitor-General of Spain?

ANSWERS ON PAGE 284

# QUIZ 176

**1 MOVIES**

In which 1988 romantic comedy did Melanie Griffith star with Harrison Ford?

**2 MUSIC**

Which singer had four Top 40 hits in the 1980s with her band the Miami Sound Machine?

**3 TV AND RADIO**

Which comic writing partnership was responsible for *Hancock's Half Hour*?

**4 SPORT AND LEISURE**

Which snooker player was world champion six times in the 1980s?

**5 GEOGRAPHY**

Of which European principality is Vaduz the capital?

**6 SCIENCE AND NATURE**

What is unique about 'monotreme' mammals?

**7 LITERATURE**

Who wrote *Swallows and Amazons*?

**8 CELEBRITIES**

Which author does Johnny Depp play in the movie *Finding Neverland*?

**9 WORDS**

A 'knobkerrie' is an African what?
- a) animal
- b) weapon
- c) hut

**10 POT LUCK**

Where in the body are the intercostal muscles?

ANSWERS ON PAGE 284

# QUIZ 177

**1  MOVIES**
Kate Winslet starred in the 1994 film *Heavenly Creatures*. Who was the director?

**2  MUSIC**
'Ghost Town' was a Number One hit in 1981 for which group?

**3  TV AND RADIO**
Rod Serling was the host and narrator of which cult TV show in the 1960s?

**4  SPORT AND LEISURE**
How was boxer Rocco Francis Marchegiano better known?

**5  HISTORY**
In which year did the Bastille fall, precipitating the French Revolution?

**6  GEOGRAPHY**
In which ocean is the island group Tuvalu?

**7  LITERATURE**
*Vernon God Little* by D B C Pierre won the Booker Prize in 2003. What do the initials 'D B C' stand for?

**8  SCIENCE AND NATURE**
Which fruit-bearing plant is scientifically known as *Cucurbita maxima*?

**9  WORDS**
What sort of a sensation is 'urtication'?
> a) wet
> b) stinging
> c) cold

**10  POT LUCK**
In which country is the port of Fremantle?

ANSWERS ON PAGE 284

# QUIZ 178

**1  MOVIES**
Which was the first *Halloween* movie not to star Jamie Lee Curtis?

**2  MUSIC**
'Do You Love Me' and 'Silence is Golden' were UK Number One hits for which group?

**3  TV AND RADIO**
Who played Ken Boon in *Boon*?

**4  SPORT AND LEISURE**
Which Scottish football team is nicknamed 'Blue Brazil'?

**5  HISTORY**
Which Massachusetts town was famously home to the 1692 witch hunts?

**6  SCIENCE AND NATURE**
Dry ice is the solid form of which gas?

**7  LITERATURE**
Who wrote *Interview with the Vampire* and *Queen of the Damned*?

**8  CELEBRITIES**
'Don't Speak' was a UK Number One for which band, featuring Gwen Stefani on vocals?

**9  WORDS**
What is a 'lanugo'?
  a) a tropical island
  b) a punctuation mark
  c) a layer of fine hair

**10  POT LUCK**
In which country would you find the Alhambra?

ANSWERS ON PAGE 284

# QUIZ 179

**1  MOVIES**

Which US comedian, who made his film debut in 1915, was originally called William Claude Dukenfield?

**2  MUSIC**

Which bizarre duo had hits in 2000 with 'Ooh Stick You!' and 'Ugly'?

**3  TV AND RADIO**

What was the name of the pantomime horse in *Rentaghost*?

**4  SPORT AND LEISURE**

Which Indian cricketer led his country to victory in the 1983 World Cup?

**5  HISTORY**

In which country was the Rosetta stone discovered?

**6  GEOGRAPHY**

What is the name of the volcanic island between Java and Sumatra?

**7  LITERATURE**

Which fictional country was the satirical creation of Samuel Butler?

**8  SCIENCE AND NATURE**

Cardiology is the medical science concerned with which organ?

**9  WORDS**

'Triskaidekaphobia' is a fear of what?

> a) ghosts
> b) the number 13
> c) the devil

**10  POT LUCK**

In semaphore, which letter is signalled when each arm is stretched out from the body horizontally?

ANSWERS ON PAGE 284

# QUIZ 180

**1  MOVIES**
Who played Hot Lips Houlihan in the 1970 movie *M\*A\*S\*H*?

**2  MUSIC**
'In the Air Tonight' was the first solo hit for which singer?

**3  TV AND RADIO**
Which *Blue Peter* presenter had a dog called Shep?

**4  SPORT AND LEISURE**
How many cards are there in a tarot deck?

**5  GEOGRAPHY**
Beatrix and Juliana are the two most recent monarchs of which European country?

**6  SCIENCE AND NATURE**
The Transbay Bridge is a feature of which US city?

**7  LITERATURE**
Who wrote the crime novels featuring Tommy and Tuppence Beresford?

**8  CELEBRITIES**
Michelle Pfeiffer, Susan Sarandon and Cher played the Witches of Eastwick in the movie of the same name. Who played Daryl van Horne?

**9  WORDS**
To 'mamaguy' means to do what?
        a) give birth
        b) chew
        c) deceive

**10  POT LUCK**
What is an 'Eton crop'?

ANSWERS ON PAGE 284

# QUIZ 181

**1 MOVIES**

David Lynch directed a movie adaptation of which Frank Herbert sci-fi novel?

**2 MUSIC**

Kerry Katona was an original member of which chart-topping female trio?

**3 TV AND RADIO**

In the US TV sitcom *Roseanne*, who played Roseanne's husband?

**4 SPORT AND LEISURE**

The modern pentathlon consists of horse riding, running, shooting, swimming and which other discipline?

**5 HISTORY**

In which year did British women over the age of 30 first get the right to vote?

**6 SCIENCE AND NATURE**

What is measured by the Beaufort scale?

**7 LITERATURE**

*Oroonoko* was a novel by possibly England's first professional female writer. What was her name?

**8 CELEBRITIES**

Kate Beckinsale starred with Hugh Jackman in which monster movie of 2004?

**9 WORDS**

'Pleonasm' is the deployment of too many what?
- a) blood cells
- b) weapons
- c) words

**10 POT LUCK**

Joseph Hobson Jagger became renowned in music hall song as the man who broke the bank where?

ANSWERS ON PAGE 285

# QUIZ 182

**1 MOVIES**
Who played the president in the 1995 movie *The American President*?

**2 MUSIC**
Jazz legend Django Reinhardt played the guitar, banjo and which other instrument?

**3 TV AND RADIO**
Which mythical Chinese hero was 'born from an egg on a mountain top' according to the 1970s TV series theme tune?

**4 SPORT AND LEISURE**
Which British city hosted the 1986 Commonwealth Games?

**5 HISTORY**
The actress Nell Gwynn was mistress to which British king?

**6 SCIENCE AND NATURE**
Which organ of the body secretes bile?

**7 LITERATURE**
Monica Ali made the 2003 Booker shortlist for which novel?

**8 CELEBRITIES**
Sean Connery was an ageing Robin Hood, but who played Maid Marian in the 1976 movie *Robin and Marian*?

**9 WORDS**
A 'kris' is a Malayan what?
> a) dish
> b) knife
> c) shoe

**10 POT LUCK**
Which historical character was also known as the 'Maid of Orleans'?

ANSWERS ON PAGE 285

# QUIZ 183

**1  MOVIES**

Who directed and starred with Janet Leigh in *Touch of Evil* in 1958?

**2  MUSIC**

Tony Orlando had a hit with 'Tie a Yellow Ribbon' as a member of which group?

**3  TV AND RADIO**

In which medical drama does Hugh Lawrie play an antisocial doctor?

**4  SPORT AND LEISURE**

What was the US sprinter Flo-Jo's full name?

**5  HISTORY**

Who was the first European to visit Trinidad and Venezuela in 1498?

**6  SCIENCE AND NATURE**

*Patella vulgata* is the Latin name of which sea creature?

**7  LITERATURE**

Cassio and Iago feature in which of Shakespeare's plays?

**8  CELEBRITIES**

Which actor, famous for his role as a wise old wizard in a series of blockbuster movies, appeared on stage in Stratford in 2007 as King Lear?

**9  WORDS**

'Psephology' is the study of what?
- a) bumps on the head
- b) elections
- c) psychic phenomena

**10  POT LUCK**

What do the initials BAFTA stand for?

ANSWERS ON PAGE 285

# QUIZ 184

**1 MOVIES**
Kim Basinger won a best supporting actress Oscar for which celebrated film noir of the 1990s?

**2 MUSIC**
Which group won a Grammy in 1979 for their song 'What a Fool Believes'?

**3 TV AND RADIO**
*Jimmy's* was a documentary set in St James's Hospital in which English city?

**4 SPORT AND LEISURE**
Which Italian team did Maradona play for?

**5 GEOGRAPHY**
What nationality was Vitus Bering, discoverer of the Bering Strait?

**6 SCIENCE AND NATURE**
What creature is depicted by the constellation Cygnus?

**7 LITERATURE**
Which Pulitzer prize-winning Alice Walker novel was filmed by Steven Spielberg?

**8 CELEBRITIES**
Natascha McElhone starred with George Clooney in which sci-fi movie remake?

**9 WORDS**
What is a 'solecism'?
> a) a skin growth
> b) a mistake
> c) an astronomical phenomenon

**10 POT LUCK**
Which award was instituted by the reigning monarch in 1856 to reward conspicuous bravery in combat?

ANSWERS ON PAGE 285

# QUIZ 185

**1 MOVIES**
Which two brothers from Minnesota have made films including *Fargo, O Brother, Where Art Thou?* and *The Man Who Wasn't There?*

**2 MUSIC**
Which group had Number One hits in 1996 with 'Killing Me Softly' and 'Ready or Not'?

**3 TV AND RADIO**
Which warrior princess was played by Lucy Lawless?

**4 SPORT AND LEISURE**
Where were the 2006 winter Olympic Games held?

**5 HISTORY**
Which king was defeated at the Battle of Hastings?

**6 SCIENCE AND NATURE**
Which metal has the symbol Fe?

**7 LITERATURE**
Who became the Poet Laureate in May 1999?

**8 CELEBRITIES**
Ray Winstone played which role in the 1980s TV series *Robin of Sherwood*?

**9 WORDS**
If something is 'cepaceous', what vegetable does it taste like?
a) a parsnip
b) an onion
c) a carrot

**10 POT LUCK**
Which RAF rank comes between squadron leader and group captain?

ANSWERS ON PAGE 285

# QUIZ 186

**1 MOVIES**
Jane Fonda starred as which spacegoing heroine in 1968?

**2 MUSIC**
J P Richardson, whose only British hit was 'Chantilly Lace' in 1958, was better known by what name?

**3 TV AND RADIO**
Which impressionist and comedian was born Robert Nankeville in 1959?

**4 SPORT AND LEISURE**
How many numbered segments are there on a standard European roulette wheel?

**5 GEOGRAPHY**
By which country is the republic of San Marino completely surrounded?

**6 SCIENCE AND NATURE**
Which planetary body has a satellite called Charon?

**7 LITERATURE**
Who wrote *Farewell, My Lovely* and *The Big Sleep*?

**8 CELEBRITIES**
Charlize Theron appears as which real-life character in the movie *The Life and Death of Peter Sellers*?

**9 WORDS**
What is piri-piri?
        a) a spicy sauce
        b) a tropical disease
        c) an Aboriginal gathering

**10 POT LUCK**
Who killed the Minotaur?

ANSWERS ON PAGE 285

# QUIZ 187

**1  MOVIES**
Rosalind Russell and Cary Grant starred in which movie version of the play *The Front Page*?

**2  MUSIC**
Which instrument did jazz musician Bill Evans play?

**3  TV AND RADIO**
Who wrote the Inspector Morse novels?

**4  SPORT AND LEISURE**
What is the British term for the game that in North America is called checkers?

**5  HISTORY**
In which year did the Church of England first ordain women priests?

**6  SCIENCE AND NATURE**
After which Scottish engineer is the SI unit of power named?

**7  ART**
Which artist painted *The Night Watch* in 1642?

**8  CELEBRITIES**
To which comedian is Jennifer Saunders married?

**9  WORDS**
If something is 'suaveolent', is it?
> a) smooth
> b) graceful
> c) fragrant

**10  POT LUCK**
Which of the Seven Wonders of the World was built at Ephesus?

ANSWERS ON PAGE 286

189

# QUIZ 188

**1  MOVIES**
Judy Garland starred as Dorothy in *The Wizard Of Oz*, but what was the name of her character's dog?

**2  MUSIC**
Which composer wrote the theme for *The Magnificent Seven*?

**3  TV AND RADIO**
*Going Straight* was a short-lived sequel to which TV series?

**4  SPORT AND LEISURE**
According to legend, the Greek runner Pheidippides was the inspiration for which sporting event?

**5  GEOGRAPHY**
People from which US state are known as 'Bay Staters'?

**6  SCIENCE AND NATURE**
Which item, still used in chemistry, was devised by Mendeleyev in 1869?

**7  LITERATURE**
Who wrote the light-hearted account of scientific thought called *A Short History of Nearly Everything*?

**8  CELEBRITIES**
What is the surname of former Spice Girl Mel C?

**9  WORDS**
What does a 'toxophilite' enjoy?
- a) snakes
- b) economics
- c) archery

**10  POT LUCK**
What does NATO stand for?

ANSWERS ON PAGE 286

# QUIZ 189

**1 MOVIES**
In which James Bond film did Honor Blackman play Pussy Galore?

**2 MUSIC**
How many strings are there on a standard acoustic guitar?

**3 TV AND RADIO**
Peter Perfect, Rufus Ruffcut and Pat Pending regularly competed against each other in which cartoon?

**4 SPORT AND LEISURE**
Which US city is home to the Redskins football team?

**5 HISTORY**
In which war did the 1968 Tet offensive occur?

**6 SCIENCE AND NATURE**
What number is denoted by the Roman numerals XC?

**7 LITERATURE**
Who wrote *Gulliver's Travels*?

**8 CELEBRITIES**
Helena Bonham Carter starred in *Planet of the Apes* and *Big Fish*, both directed by her partner. What is his name?

**9 WORDS**
What sort of animal is an 'albacore'?
- a) a horse
- b) a bird
- c) a fish

**10 POT LUCK**
In *Thunderbirds*, what is the name of Lady Penelope's chauffeur?

ANSWERS ON PAGE 286

# QUIZ 190

**1 MOVIES**
*Blue Juice*, *Big Wednesday* and *Point Break* are movies featuring which sport?

**2 MUSIC**
'My Generation', 'Substitute' and 'Won't Get Fooled Again' were Top Ten hits for which group?

**3 TV AND RADIO**
Perkin, Posie and Pootle featured in which animated 1970s TV series?

**4 SPORT AND LEISURE**
In which sport did Sandy Koufax excel?

**5 HISTORY**
Which king ruled England from 1042 to 1066?

**6 SCIENCE AND NATURE**
Which German-born scientist formulated the theories of Special and General Relativity?

**7 LITERATURE**
C Auguste Dupin, the original sleuth, was created by which writer?

**8 CELEBRITIES**
What was the 1987 vampire movie that starred Kiefer Sutherland and Dianne Wiest?

**9 WORDS**
What did a 'wainwright' make?
- a) guns
- b) barrels
- c) wagons

**10 POT LUCK**
Which imaginary world was created by L Frank Baum?

ANSWERS ON PAGE 286

# QUIZ 191

ANSWERS ON PAGE 286

**1 MOVIES**
How many of the original Beatles did voice-overs for the animated movie *Yellow Submarine*?

**2 MUSIC**
Siouxsie was the lead singer for which punk band?

**3 TV AND RADIO**
Which number was assigned to 'the Prisoner' in the 1960s show of the same name?

**4 SPORT AND LEISURE**
What is the minimum length of an international football pitch?

**5 HISTORY**
Between 1972 and 1975, of which country was Edward Gough Whitlam the prime minister?

**6 SCIENCE AND NATURE**
Who invented the C5 personal transport vehicle?

**7 LITERATURE**
Which author won the Booker Prize for *The Remains of the Day*?

**8 CELEBRITIES**
Scarlett Johansson starred in a movie adaptation of which Tracy Chevalier novel?

**9 WORDS**
The word 'ubiquitous' describes something which is where?
- a) nowhere
- b) everywhere
- c) somewhere

**10 POT LUCK**
In the common saying, which animal might one be as bald as?

# QUIZ 192

**1  MOVIES**

Hilary Swank starred with Aaron Eckhart and Stanley Tucci in which improbable disaster movie?

**2  MUSIC**

'Twenty Four Hours from Tulsa' and 'Something's Gotten Hold of My Heart' were Top Ten hits for whom?

**3  TV AND RADIO**

In the BBC comedy *Up Pompeii!*, who played Lurcio?

**4  SPORT AND LEISURE**

Which football team is nicknamed 'the Toffees'?

**5  HISTORY**

Which British monarch died in 1901?

**6  SCIENCE AND NATURE**

What kind of animal is a 'mandrill'?

**7  LITERATURE**

What is the name of the lion in *The Lion, the Witch and the Wardrobe*?

**8  CELEBRITIES**

Which celebrity did the salsa singer Marc Anthony marry in June 2004?

**9  WORDS**

A 'bellicose' person is what?
a) ravenous
b) warlike
c) beautiful

**10  POT LUCK**

Roger Mellie and Sid the Sexist are characters in which comic?

ANSWERS ON PAGE 286

# QUIZ 193

**1  MOVIES**
Audrey Tautou lit up which 2001 Jean-Pierre Jeunet movie?

**2  MUSIC**
*La donna è mobile* comes from which Verdi opera?

**3  TV AND RADIO**
Who starred as Steve Baxter in ITV's 2002 drama *The Second Coming*?

**4  SPORT AND LEISURE**
How many chess pieces are on the board at the start of a game?

**5  HISTORY**
Which document was sealed at Runnymede in 1215?

**6  SCIENCE AND NATURE**
Which element has the symbol Pb?

**7  ART**
Which artist painted *Blue Boy* and *The Harvest Wagon*?

**8  CELEBRITIES**
Calista Flockhart starred as Helena in which Shakespearean movie adaptation of 1999?

**9  WORDS**
An animal about to 'aestivate' is going to do what?
   a) shed its fur
   b) produce young
   c) sleep all summer

**10  POT LUCK**
Which Hollywood star wrote an autobiography called *My Wicked Wicked Ways*?

ANSWERS ON PAGE 287

# QUIZ 194

**1  MOVIES**
Who played Lee Harvey Oswald in Oliver Stone's *JFK*?

**2  MUSIC**
Which musician provided the soundtracks for the movies *Cal* and *Local Hero*?

**3  TV AND RADIO**
Gaby Roslin, Paula Yates, Zoe Ball and Sharron Davies all worked as presenters on which 1990s Channel 4 morning show?

**4  SPORT AND LEISURE**
Which sport takes place in a lane roughly 105cm/42in wide and 18m/60ft long?

**5  HISTORY**
Which US president immediately preceded Ronald Reagan?

**6  SCIENCE AND NATURE**
How many square metres are there in a hectare?

**7  LITERATURE**
Which author's novels include *Quite Ugly One Morning* and *Boiling a Frog*?

**8  CELEBRITIES**
Rula Lenska played Nancy 'Q' Cunard de Longchamps in which TV series of the 1970s?

**9  WORDS**
What would you do with a 'tallit'?
> a) eat it
> b) ride it
> c) wear it

**10  POT LUCK**
Which newspaper is also facetiously known as 'The Thunderer'?

ANSWERS ON PAGE 287

# QUIZ 195

**1 MOVIES**

Which famous disaster features in the movie *A Night to Remember*?

**2 MUSIC**

Who composed the 'New World' symphony?

**3 TV AND RADIO**

Patrick Troughton and Peter Davison were the second and fifth incarnations of which television character?

**4 SPORT AND LEISURE**

In which board game do Professor Plum and Colonel Mustard feature?

**5 HISTORY**

Of which South American civilization was Atahualpa an emperor?

**6 SCIENCE AND NATURE**

Which unit, used to measure horses, is 10cm/4in in extent?

**7 LITERATURE**

Which playwright wrote *Can't Pay? Won't Pay!* and *Accidental Death of an Anarchist*?

**8 CELEBRITIES**

Ally Sheedy starred with Matthew Broderick in which 1983 computer paranoia movie?

**9 WORDS**

What is a 'pilliwinks'?
- a) an instrument of torture
- b) an unusually short finger or thumb
- c) a quick nap in the afternoon

**10 POT LUCK**

What was the name of the first horse in *Steptoe and Son*?

ANSWERS ON PAGE 287

# QUIZ 196

**1  MOVIES**
Tom Hanks and Paul Newman appeared in which 2002 gangster movie?

**2  MUSIC**
Which band, fronted by Eddi Reader, had a UK Number One with 'Perfect' in 1988?

**3  TV AND RADIO**
Who lived with Sid James at 23 Railway Cuttings, East Cheam?

**4  SPORT AND LEISURE**
The world's first organized bobsleigh competition took place in 1898 on which Swiss course?

**5  GEOGRAPHY**
Honduras has coastlines on the Caribbean Sea and which other body of water?

**6  SCIENCE AND NATURE**
What is the unit of measurement of luminous intensity, abbreviated to cd?

**7  ART**
Which sculptor's works include *The Age of Bronze*, *The Gates of Hell*, *The Kiss*, *The Thinker* and *The Burghers of Calais*?

**8  LITERATURE**
Shere Khan appears in which of Rudyard Kipling's books?

**9  WORDS**
'Scutellation' describes the arrangement of what?
- a) animal scales
- b) sunken ships
- c) sprinkled salt

**10  POT LUCK**
What is the traditional cry given when a huntsman catches sight of the fox?

ANSWERS ON PAGE 287

# QUIZ 197

**1  MOVIES**
In which 1995 movie did Al Pacino finally get to share a scene with Robert De Niro?

**2  MUSIC**
'I Heard It Through The Grapevine' and '(Sexual) Healing' were hits for which singer?

**3  TV AND RADIO**
Which character was played by Jason Alexander in *Seinfeld*?

**4  SPORT AND LEISURE**
In which game would you encounter a 'roquet', a 'tice' and might you 'peg out' or 'wire'?

**5  HISTORY**
When did America adopt the Declaration of Independence?

**6  SCIENCE AND NATURE**
Which imperial quantity is about equal to 4.55 litres?

**7  LITERATURE**
Which poet and novelist was portrayed by Gwyneth Paltrow in the movie *Sylvia*?

**8  CELEBRITIES**
For which 1991 Martin Scorsese film did Juliette Lewis receive an Oscar nomination?

**9  WORDS**
When does a 'quinquennial' event occur?
> a) every five years
> b) every 15 years
> c) every 50 years

**10  POT LUCK**
Which material represents your 14th wedding anniversary?

ANSWERS ON PAGE 287

# QUIZ 198

**1 MOVIES**
In which 2005 children's film did Tilda Swinton play the villainess?

**2 MUSIC**
Which US composer wrote *Fanfare for the Common Man*?

**3 TV AND RADIO**
In which city is *Casualty* set?

**4 SPORT AND LEISURE**
Which game was played by Boris Spassky?

**5 HISTORY**
In which war was the Battle of Balaclava fought?

**6 SCIENCE AND NATURE**
Where in Ukraine did a nuclear reactor explode disastrously in 1986?

**7 ART**
A bronze statue worth £3 million that was stolen from the grounds of a Hertfordshire museum in December 2005 was by which sculptor?

**8 CELEBRITIES**
Faye Dunaway starred opposite which leading actor in the original movie *The Thomas Crown Affair*?

**9 WORDS**
In ancient Rome, what was a 'sesterce'?
- a) a coin
- b) a bodyguard
- c) a temple

**10 POT LUCK**
'Baily's beads' can be glimpsed briefly during which phenomenon?

ANSWERS ON PAGE 287

# QUIZ 199

**1 MOVIES**
Which sci-fi movie was first filmed in 1955 starring Kevin McCarthy, and was then remade in 1978 with Donald Sutherland, Jeff Goldblum and Leonard Nimoy?

**2 MUSIC**
What was Blondie's first UK chart hit?

**3 TV AND RADIO**
Jack Lord was the star of which glamorous 1970s cop show?

**4 SPORT AND LEISURE**
In which sport was the US athlete Don Budge a champion?

**5 HISTORY**
How was Mexican revolutionary Francisco Villa better known?

**6 GEOGRAPHY**
Of which country is Kampala the capital city?

**7 LITERATURE**
Who writes novels about a detective called Adam Dalgleish?

**8 SCIENCE AND NATURE**
Which birds are described as 'strigiform'?

**9 WORDS**
What does a 'mesocephalic' person have?
- a) a small head
- b) a medium-sized head
- c) a big head

**10 POT LUCK**
With which city does the M11 link London?

ANSWERS ON PAGE 288

# QUIZ 200

**1 MOVIES**
Who composed the distinctive score for *The Third Man*?

**2 MUSIC**
With which popular Scandinavian group was Marie Fredriksson the singer?

**3 TV AND RADIO**
Dr Sabatini and Dr Haslam were characters in which hospital-based ITV sitcom?

**4 SPORT AND LEISURE**
In which year did Sir Stanley Matthews die?

**5 GEOGRAPHY**
In which country is the city of Mombasa?

**6 SCIENCE AND NATURE**
How many nautical miles are in a nautical league?

**7 LITERATURE**
Which Greek dramatist wrote *Medea* and *Electra*?

**8 CELEBRITIES**
Billy Connolly starred as Zebulon Gant in which 2003 movie?

**9 WORDS**
What is 'speleology' the study of?
- a) magic
- b) grammar
- c) caves

**10 POT LUCK**
Who composed the opera *Don Giovanni*?

ANSWERS ON PAGE 288

# QUIZ 201

**1   MOVIES**
Which Monty Python star played Robin Hood in *The Time Bandits*?

**2   MUSIC**
Who had chart hits with 'Gertcha', 'Rabbit' and 'Snooker Loopy'?

**3   TV AND RADIO**
Who became the director-general of the BBC in May 2004?

**4   SPORT AND LEISURE**
Which British athlete was the Olympic 1,500m gold medallist in 1980 and 1984?

**5   HISTORY**
Who captained *The Bounty* until the famous mutiny occurred?

**6   GEOGRAPHY**
The balboa is the unit of currency in which central American country?

**7   LITERATURE**
Who wrote *Raise the Titanic*, *Atlantis Found* and other novels featuring rugged hero Dirk Pitt?

**8   SCIENCE AND NATURE**
Where in the human body would you find the femur?

**9   WORDS**
What shape is something described as 'flabellate'?
- a) fan-shaped
- b) bottle-shaped
- c) needle-shaped

**10   POT LUCK**
Who was the first woman MP to sit in the House of Commons?

ANSWERS ON PAGE 288

# QUIZ 202

**1 MOVIES**
Who directed the 1946 James Stewart movie *It's a Wonderful Life*?

**2 MUSIC**
Which singer and pianist was born Barry Pincus in 1946?

**3 TV AND RADIO**
What was the name of the toad in *Bagpuss*?

**4 SPORT AND LEISURE**
Which English football team plays at the Stadium of Light?

**5 GEOGRAPHY**
In which ocean are the Marshall Islands?

**6 SCIENCE AND NATURE**
What is 'chromatics' the science of?

**7 LITERATURE**
For which book is Yann Martel most famous?

**8 CELEBRITIES**
Which video game character has Angelina Jolie played twice on screen?

**9 WORDS**
Where would you find a 'picador'?
   a) in a fencing match
   b) in a bullfight
   c) in a game of badminton

**10 POT LUCK**
In the Old Testament, which Philistine was killed by David?

ANSWERS ON PAGE 288

# QUIZ 203

**1   MOVIES**
Karen Allen was the heroine of which 1981 Indiana Jones movie?

**2   MUSIC**
What is the surname of the clean-shaven drummer in hairy rock group ZZ Top?

**3   TV AND RADIO**
Richard Griffiths played culinary sleuth Henry Crabbe in which BBC TV series of the 1990s?

**4   SPORT AND LEISURE**
Which Czech athlete won gold medals in the 1952 Olympics for the 5,000m, the 10,000m and the marathon?

**5   HISTORY**
Who succeeded Winston Churchill as British prime minister in 1955?

**6   GEOGRAPHY**
Nicosia is the capital of which Mediterranean island?

**7   LITERATURE**
What are the first names of the literary characters Dr Jekyll and Mr Hyde?

**8   SCIENCE AND NATURE**
Agra Fort and the Taj Mahal are world heritage sites in which country?

**9   WORDS**
What does a 'sphygmomanometer' measure?
  a) rainfall
  b) wood density
  c) blood pressure

**10   POT LUCK**
Which former US vice president was the subject of the documentary film *An Inconvenient Truth*?

ANSWERS ON PAGE 288

# QUIZ 204

1   **MOVIES**
In the 1938 *The Adventures of Robin Hood*, which role was played by Basil Rathbone?

2   **MUSIC**
Which Russian composed *The Firebird*?

3   **TV AND RADIO**
What is Marge Simpson's maiden name?

4   **SPORT AND LEISURE**
Which Brit became motor racing Grand Prix champion in 1976 and died in 1993?

5   **GEOGRAPHY**
Which US state is known as the 'Diamond state'?

6   **SCIENCE AND NATURE**
What is the seventh planet out from the Sun?

7   **LITERATURE**
What condition besets the narrator of Mark Haddon's novel *The Curious Incident of the Dog in the Night Time*?

8   **CELEBRITIES**
Which comic book heroine did Pamela Anderson play in a 1996 movie?

9   **WORDS**
What is a 'hirsute' person?
                a) mad
                b) hairy
                c) strong

10   **POT LUCK**
Which infectious throat disease is named after the Greek word for leather?

ANSWERS ON PAGE 288

# QUIZ 205

**1 MOVIES**
Anne Heche starred with Al Pacino and Johnny Depp in which 1997 crime movie?

**2 MUSIC**
How was singer and musician Simon John Ritchie better known?

**3 TV AND RADIO**
Who replaced Meg Foster as Cagney in TV cop show *Cagney and Lacey*?

**4 SPORT AND LEISURE**
Which city hosted the summer Olympic Games in 1980?

**5 HISTORY**
In 1411 the first university in Scotland was established. Where?

**6 SCIENCE AND NATURE**
Scafell Pike is the highest point in which UK national park?

**7 LITERATURE**
Which US novelist wrote *Gravity's Rainbow*?

**8 CELEBRITIES**
Which singer and television presenter was born Priscilla White in 1943?

**9 WORDS**
If something is 'amaranthine', what colour is it?
- a) dark blue
- b) dark green
- c) dark purple-red

**10 POT LUCK**
What was the name of Dick Turpin's horse?

ANSWERS ON PAGE 289

# QUIZ 206

**1 MOVIES**

*THX 1138* was the first feature-length movie by which prominent film-maker?

**2 MUSIC**

'Car Wash' and 'Love Don't Live Here Anymore' were 1970s hits for which group?

**3 TV AND RADIO**

Susan Stranks, Jenny Hanley and Tony Bastable all hosted which ITV equivalent of *Blue Peter*?

**4 SPORT AND LEISURE**

How many points does the 'outer' on a dart board score?

**5 HISTORY**

In the Six Day War in 1967, which country defeated an alliance of Egypt, Syria and Jordan?

**6 SCIENCE AND NATURE**

The name of which seabird, of the genus Morus, is also slang for a greedy person?

**7 ART**

In which city would you find the Uffizi gallery?

**8 CELEBRITIES**

Of which movie director is Bryce Dallas Howard the daughter?

**9 WORDS**

With reference to insects, what is an 'ootheca'?
- a) a feeler
- b) a digestive tract
- c) an egg capsule

**10 POT LUCK**

In which city would you find the Sorbonne university?

ANSWERS ON PAGE 289

# QUIZ 207

**1  MOVIES**
Who provided the voice of the Fairy Godmother in *Shrek 2*?

**2  MUSIC**
Who had UK Top Ten hits with 'Dancing in the Dark', 'I'm on Fire' and 'Streets of Philadelphia'?

**3  TV AND RADIO**
*ITMA* was one of the most popular radio programmes of the 1940s. What did the initials ITMA stand for?

**4  SPORT AND LEISURE**
How many points are awarded for a try in Rugby League?

**5  GEOGRAPHY**
What is the capital of the Isle of Man?

**6  SCIENCE AND NATURE**
What is nitrous oxide better known as?

**7  ART**
With which Spanish film director did Salvador Dalí collaborate on the surrealist films *Un Chien Andalou* in 1928 and *L'Age d'or* in 1930?

**8  LITERATURE**
Who wrote *Scoop* and *Brideshead Revisited*?

**9  WORDS**
A 'venal' person is what?
> a) mean
> b) blood-spattered
> c) mercenary

**10  POT LUCK**
What nationality is the chef on *The Muppet Show*?

ANSWERS ON PAGE 289

# QUIZ 208

**1  MOVIES**
Sharon Stone starred with Robert De Niro and Joe Pesci in which Martin Scorsese movie?

**2  MUSIC**
Which US songwriter wrote the song 'Send in the Clowns'?

**3  TV AND RADIO**
How much did it cost to turn astronaut Steve Austin into a bionic man?

**4  SPORT AND LEISURE**
Which jockey won the Derby on Troy in 1979 and Henbit in 1980?

**5  HISTORY**
What name was given to supporters of James VII and II, and his successors?

**6  SCIENCE AND NATURE**
What are the four groups into which human blood is usually classified?

**7  ART**
Which Yorkshire sculptor is famous for *Figure of a Woman* and *Single Form*?

**8  CELEBRITIES**
Which comic villain did Uma Thurman play in *Batman and Robin*?

**9  WORDS**
What does 'mephitic' mean?
  a) magical
  b) foul
  c) blessed

**10  POT LUCK**
'Growlers' and 'bergybits' are types of what?

ANSWERS ON PAGE 289

# QUIZ 209

**1  MOVIES**
Elsa Lanchester was the bride of whom in a 1935 movie?

**2  MUSIC**
Which US group had hits with 'Hold the Line', 'Africa' and 'Rosanna'?

**3  TV AND RADIO**
Who played Polly in *Fawlty Towers*?

**4  SPORT AND LEISURE**
Dutch football team Ajax is at home in which city?

**5  GEOGRAPHY**
Archbishop Makarios III was president of which country from 1960 to 1977?

**6  SCIENCE AND NATURE**
What was Thomas Edison's middle name?

**7  ART**
Which US artist famously declared that 'in the future everybody will be world famous for 15 minutes'?

**8  CELEBRITIES**
Who played PJ in *Byker Grove*?

**9  WORDS**
'Embracery' is a criminal attempt to influence whom?
   a) a politician
   b) a jury
   c) a policeman

**10  POT LUCK**
How is Barbara Millicent Roberts better known?

ANSWERS ON PAGE 289

# QUIZ 210

**1  MOVIES**

Which movie's poster proclaimed 'In Space No One Can Hear You Scream'?

**2  MUSIC**

What was the one-word title of Sabrina's 1988 novelty hit which had the subtitle 'Summertime Love'?

**3  TV AND RADIO**

Who hosted *University Challenge* before Jeremy Paxman?

**4  SPORT AND LEISURE**

What is the green material covering a billiard table called?

**5  HISTORY**

From which country did the soldier and politician Moshe Dayan come?

**6  SCIENCE AND NATURE**

By what name was the hoax hominid skeleton found in Sussex in 1912 known?

**7  LITERATURE**

Raskolnikov is the central character in which Russian novel?

**8  CELEBRITIES**

Helen Mirren starred in which 1984 movie based on a novel by Bernard MacLaverty?

**9  WORDS**

A 'pusillanimous' person lacks what, specifically?
- a) courage
- b) money
- c) blood

**10  POT LUCK**

According to the rhyme, a child born on which day has far to go?

ANSWERS ON PAGE 289

# QUIZ 211

**1  MOVIES**
Which character does Cate Blanchett play in the *Lord of the Rings* films?

**2  MUSIC**
Who took a cover version of Bob Dylan's 'Mr Tambourine Man' to Number One in 1965?

**3  TV AND RADIO**
For which comedian was the sitcom *Up the Elephant and Round the Castle* written?

**4  SPORT AND LEISURE**
Swimming and running are two of the disciplines in the triathlon. What is the third?

**5  GEOGRAPHY**
What is the capital city of Trinidad and Tobago?

**6  SCIENCE AND NATURE**
An 'eft' is what sort of animal?

**7  LITERATURE**
What were novelist D H Lawrence's first two names?

**8  CELEBRITIES**
Liz Hurley starred in a remake of which Pete and Dud movie?

**9  WORDS**
If you 'lucubrate', by what do you study?
            a) post
            b) observation
            c) lamplight

**10  POT LUCK**
What is the name of the Japanese religion that incorporates ancestor worship?

ANSWERS ON PAGE 290

# QUIZ 212

**1 MOVIES**
In the film *McVicar*, which rock singer played the eponymous criminal?

**2 MUSIC**
The Skatalites had a hit in 1967 with a ska cover version of which movie theme?

**3 TV AND RADIO**
Samantha Janus played Mandy Wilkins in which TV sitcom?

**4 SPORT AND LEISURE**
Swede Tony Rickardsson has been world champion five times in which sport?

**5 HISTORY**
Which US frontiersman, born in 1786, died fighting for Texas at the Battle of the Alamo?

**6 SCIENCE AND NATURE**
Professor Dumbledore in the *Harry Potter* stories shares his name with a dialect word for which insect?

**7 ART**
Who became famous for his photographs of Yosemite national park, California, in the 1930s?

**8 CELEBRITIES**
With whom did Mary J Blige record the single 'As' in 1999?

**9 WORDS**
'Bastinado' is a form of what?
        a) torture
        b) handicraft
        c) woodwind music

**10 POT LUCK**
Knut, rejected by his mother and hand-raised by his keeper at Berlin Zoo, became a German celebrity in 2007. What kind of animal was he?

ANSWERS ON PAGE 290

# QUIZ 213

**1 MOVIES**

The 1970s sci-fi film *Soylent Green* was the last movie for which legendary gangster actor?

**2 MUSIC**

Which Italian composer wrote the music for *The Good, the Bad and the Ugly* and many other spaghetti westerns?

**3 TV AND RADIO**

Whose life and times did Dan Haggerty portray on TV from 1978 to 1979?

**4 SPORT AND LEISURE**

How many players are there in a water polo team?

**5 HISTORY**

Of which country did Helen Clark become prime minister in 1999?

**6 SCIENCE AND NATURE**

Alexander Fleming is chiefly remembered for discovering which substance in 1928?

**7 ART**

Which UK city is home to the Kelvingrove Art Gallery and Museum?

**8 CELEBRITIES**

Catherine Zeta-Jones starred opposite George Clooney in which Coen brothers movie?

**9 WORDS**

What creatures does a 'herpetologist' study?
- a) birds
- b) reptiles
- c) fish

**10 POT LUCK**

Which US state is known as the 'Hoosier state'?

ANSWERS ON PAGE 290

# QUIZ 214

**1 MOVIES**
Which *Wizard of Oz* character starts the film lacking a brain?

**2 MUSIC**
Which Welsh group had a Top Ten hit in 1992 with a cover version of the 'Theme From M*A*S*H'?

**3 TV AND RADIO**
Who was the chief executive of Channel 4 from 1988 to 1997?

**4 SPORT AND LEISURE**
Who was the first person to sail non-stop and single-handed around the world?

**5 GEOGRAPHY**
Hastings Banda was a prominent politician in which African country?

**6 SCIENCE AND NATURE**
Boysenberry and loganberry are crosses between which two fruits?

**7 LITERATURE**
In which Shakespeare play would you find the characters Bottom and Puck?

**8 CELEBRITIES**
Angelina Jolie played Antonio Banderas's mail-order bride in which movie?

**9 WORDS**
A 'cubit' was originally a length measured from what to the tip of the longest finger?
> a) the nose
> b) the knee
> c) the elbow

**10 POT LUCK**
What is the 'Ship of the Desert'?

ANSWERS ON PAGE 290

# QUIZ 215

### 1 MOVIES
Which actor's first screen test was received with the comment 'Can't act. Can't sing. Can dance a little.'?

### 2 MUSIC
Patsy Kensit had a 1988 hit with 'I'm Not Scared' as part of which band?

### 3 TV AND RADIO
By what name is the Light Programme radio network now known?

### 4 SPORT AND LEISURE
In which year did Andre Agassi win the Wimbledon men's singles championship?

### 5 HISTORY
Which Macedonian king conquered Egypt in 332 BC?

### 6 SCIENCE AND NATURE
What is 0.0833 (recurring) expressed as a fraction?

### 7 LITERATURE
What was the name of Sherlock Holmes's detective partner?

### 8 CELEBRITIES
What was the title of Marilyn Monroe's last completed film?

### 9 WORDS
What does a 'sybarite' enjoy?
- a) word games
- b) killing
- c) luxury

### 10 POT LUCK
Which broadcaster is remembered for his 'Clunk click every trip' road safety adverts?

ANSWERS ON PAGE 290

# QUIZ 216

**1 MOVIES**
Who wrote, produced and directed the 1970s martial arts movie *Way of the Dragon*?

**2 MUSIC**
'Livin' La Vida Loca' was a Number One UK hit for which singer?

**3 TV AND RADIO**
Which *Neighbours* character was played by Holly Valance?

**4 SPORT AND LEISURE**
In which year did Torvill and Dean win the Olympic gold medal for ice dancing?

**5 GEOGRAPHY**
Mogadishu is the capital city of which African country?

**6 SCIENCE AND NATURE**
The tangelo is a tangerine crossed with which other sort of fruit?

**7 ART**
Which artist was the 1986 European space probe to Halley's comet named after?

**8 CELEBRITIES**
Emily Mortimer and Ewan McGregor starred in a movie adaptation of which Alexander Trocchi novel?

**9 WORDS**
A 'dirndl' is a type of what?
  a) skirt
  b) reed instrument
  c) snake

**10 POT LUCK**
Who wrote *Little Lord Fauntleroy*?

ANSWERS ON PAGE 290

# QUIZ 217

1 **MOVIES**
Which of Krzysztof Kieslowski's *Three Colours* trilogy starred Juliette Binoche?

2 **MUSIC**
Whose single 'I Feel Love' reached Number One in the UK in 1977?

3 **TV AND RADIO**
Which Gerry Anderson-created puppet defenders of the Earth were led by Tiger Ninestein?

4 **SPORT AND LEISURE**
Who rode Moonshell to victory in the Oaks in 1995?

5 **HISTORY**
In which year was the Suez crisis?

6 **SCIENCE AND NATURE**
Where would you find the Cassini division?

7 **LITERATURE**
Who wrote the children's novel *The Box of Delights*?

8 **CELEBRITIES**
What was the name of the band fronted by Courtney Love?

9 **WORDS**
What does something 'onomastic' relate to?
   a) chewing gum
   b) proper names
   c) emu farming

10 **POT LUCK**
Which word represents the letter J in the Nato alphabet?

ANSWERS ON PAGE 291

# QUIZ 218

**1   MOVIES**

Who played Nazi war criminal Dr Christian Szell in *Marathon Man*?

**2   MUSIC**

Justin Timberlake originally sang with which Florida-based boy band?

**3   TV AND RADIO**

What was the name of the dog in the 1960s children's TV show *The Herbs*?

**4   SPORT AND LEISURE**

Which country joined the five nations in 2000 to create the Six Nations Championship in Rugby Union?

**5   HISTORY**

The 19th-century British workers who destroyed newly invented textile machinery were known by what name?

**6   SCIENCE AND NATURE**

Which element has the atomic number 6?

**7   LITERATURE**

Siegfried and Tristan Farnon appear in a series of books by which vet?

**8   CELEBRITIES**

At the age of 12 Charlotte Church released her first classical album. What was it called?

**9   WORDS**

What is a 'mendicant'?
- a) a chemical preparation
- b) a beggar
- c) a politician

**10   POT LUCK**

How many blank tiles are there in a standard Scrabble® set?

ANSWERS ON PAGE 291

# QUIZ 219

**1 MOVIES**
In the 2004 movie remake of *Starsky and Hutch*, who played Hutch?

**2 MUSIC**
According to the title of Tribe of Toffs's novelty hit of 1988, who is a weatherman?

**3 TV AND RADIO**
Who played Gareth Blackstock in the TV sitcom *Chef!*?

**4 SPORT AND LEISURE**
In which sport was Welshman Richie Burnett a world champion in 1995?

**5 HISTORY**
Who was the emperor of Rome directly before Nero?

**6 SCIENCE AND NATURE**
In which US state is the Hoover Dam?

**7 LITERATURE**
Of which literary movement were Jack Kerouac, Allan Ginsberg and William Burroughs the leading lights?

**8 CELEBRITIES**
Which fiery chef called his autobiography *Humble Pie*?

**9 WORDS**
When does an 'interregnum' occur?
- a) between acts
- b) between rulers
- c) between songs

**10 POT LUCK**
What is the name of the luckless rabbit hunter in the *Bugs Bunny* cartoons?

ANSWERS ON PAGE 291

# QUIZ 220

**1 MOVIES**
Whose real name was Betty Perske?

**2 MUSIC**
'The Combine Harvester' and 'I am a Cider Drinker' were novelty hits for which group?

**3 TV AND RADIO**
Geoffrey Bayldon played which time-travelling wizard in a 1970s children's TV series?

**4 SPORT AND LEISURE**
Simon Sherwood rode which horse to victory in the 1989 Cheltenham Gold Cup?

**5 HISTORY**
Which Mongol ruler conquered Northern China in the 13th century?

**6 SCIENCE AND NATURE**
What sort of animal is a 'katydid'?

**7 LITERATURE**
Whose last and unfinished novel was *The Mystery of Edwin Drood*?

**8 CELEBRITIES**
Which character from *The Dukes of Hazzard* is played by Jessica Simpson in the movie and Catherine Bach in the TV series?

**9 WORDS**
What is a 'termagant'?
        a) a plumed wildfowl
        b) a shrewish woman
        c) a tyrannical ruler

**10 POT LUCK**
On what date is Groundhog Day commemorated in the USA?

ANSWERS ON PAGE 291

# QUIZ 221

**1  MOVIES**
Jennifer Lopez starred with George Clooney in a movie adaptation of which Elmore Leonard novel?

**2  MUSIC**
Rita Coolidge had a hit with 'All Time High', the theme from which Bond movie?

**3  TV AND RADIO**
Jason Priestley played Brandon Walsh in which early 1990s teen TV series?

**4  SPORT AND LEISURE**
Which football team is known as 'the Cottagers'?

**5  HISTORY**
In which year was the Shah of Iran deposed?

**6  SCIENCE AND NATURE**
Which US brothers, famous for making cereals, established the Battle Creek Sanatorium?

**7  LITERATURE**
Who wrote the novels *Of Mice and Men* and *The Grapes of Wrath*?

**8  CELEBRITIES**
Michelle Pfeiffer starred as singer Susie Diamond in which 1980s movie?

**9  WORDS**
What is 'saxifrage'?
>        a) a tribe
>        b) a plant
>        c) a crime

**10  POT LUCK**
Who said 'In politics, if you want anything said, ask a man. If you want anything done, ask a woman.'?

ANSWERS ON PAGE 291

# QUIZ 222

**1  MOVIES**
In which Tom Cruise movie does Demi Moore play a navy lawyer?

**2  MUSIC**
Jazz trumpeter John Birks Gillespie was better known by what nickname?

**3  TV AND RADIO**
Who played Keith in the 1970s TV show *The Partridge Family*?

**4  SPORT AND LEISURE**
Which football team won the 1990 World Cup in Italy?

**5  GEOGRAPHY**
Tashkent is the capital city of which former member of the USSR?

**6  SCIENCE AND NATURE**
An 'elver' is a young form of which animal?

**7  LITERATURE**
Mr Darcy and Elizabeth Bennett feature in which Jane Austen novel?

**8  CELEBRITIES**
Which seasoned rocker joked in a 2007 interview that he had snorted the ashes of his late father?

**9  WORDS**
'Brouhaha', a word meaning commotion, derives from which language?
>    a) Gaelic
>    b) Spanish
>    c) French

**10  POT LUCK**
In Roman mythology, which son of Jupiter was the god of fire and metal working?

ANSWERS ON PAGE 291

# QUIZ 223

**1 MOVIES**
Gort is Klaatu's robot in which 1950s sci-fi movie?

**2 MUSIC**
'The Power of Love' by Huey Lewis and the News featured prominently in which 1980s movie?

**3 TV AND RADIO**
The 1980s sitcom *Metal Mickey* was produced by which of the Monkees?

**4 SPORT AND LEISURE**
What name is given to the activity of trying to climb every Scottish mountain over 3,000 ft?

**5 GEOGRAPHY**
Which central American country borders Nicaragua to the north?

**6 SCIENCE AND NATURE**
Which founder of Microsoft wrote *The Road Ahead*?

**7 LITERATURE**
Which Norwegian dramatist wrote *Peer Gynt* and *A Doll's House*?

**8 CELEBRITIES**
Alicia Keys has had two UK Top Ten hits. What was the title of the first?

**9 WORDS**
To 'imprecate' means to what?
- a) criticize
- b) curse
- c) involve

**10 POT LUCK**
What is the smallest denomination euro note?

ANSWERS ON PAGE 292

# QUIZ 224

### 1 MOVIES
In the movie *Bringing Up Baby* starring Cary Grant and Katharine Hepburn, who or what is Baby?

### 2 MUSIC
Which US singer had hits with the themes from the movies *Fame* and *Flashdance*?

### 3 TV AND RADIO
Anneka Rice and Annabel Croft flew around the countryside in a helicopter in which Channel 4 game show?

### 4 SPORT AND LEISURE
Which Japanese art of self-defence has two disciplines called 'tomiki' and 'ueshiba'?

### 5 GEOGRAPHY
Which country's flag consists of a red disk on a white background?

### 6 SCIENCE AND NATURE
Which crop does the Colorado beetle principally damage?

### 7 LITERATURE
Under what name did Mary Ann Evans publish novels?

### 8 CELEBRITIES
Sean Bean starred in the fourth episode of which long-running UK police soap?

### 9 WORDS
What are you doing if you are 'vituperating'?
- a) secreting poison
- b) digesting food
- c) using abusive language

### 10 POT LUCK
Which band had the hits 'Monday Monday' and 'Dedicated to the One I Love'?

ANSWERS ON PAGE 292

# QUIZ 225

**1 MOVIES**
Which comedian played Sergeant Bilko in the 1990s movie of the same name?

**2 MUSIC**
Which Andrew Lloyd-Webber musical featured the songs 'Oh, What a Circus' and 'Rainbow High'?

**3 TV AND RADIO**
Peter Griffin is the oafish patriarch in which contemporary animated TV series?

**4 SPORT AND LEISURE**
In polo, how long does a chukka last?

**5 HISTORY**
Who published his *Dictionary of the English Language* in 1755?

**6 SCIENCE AND NATURE**
In which part of the body would you find the cochlea?

**7 LITERATURE**
Robert Donat and Madeleine Carroll starred in which 1930s Hitchcock movie adaptation of a John Buchan novel?

**8 CELEBRITIES**
What was the middle name of Elvis Presley?

**9 WORDS**
What are 'aurochs'?
> a) wealthy rulers
> b) extinct cattle
> c) marine stabilizers

**10 POT LUCK**
Which soap opera's first episode was broadcast on 9 December 1960?

ANSWERS ON PAGE 292

# QUIZ 226

**1   MOVIES**
What sort of giant animal links the movies *Donnie Darko* and *Harvey*?

**2   MUSIC**
'You Ain't Seen Nothing Yet' was a 1974 hit for which rock band?

**3   TV AND RADIO**
Which BBC drama series of the early 1990s followed the story of two sisters and their 1920s fashion business?

**4   SPORT AND LEISURE**
What is the name of the tree trunk traditionally tossed in the Highland Games?

**5   HISTORY**
How were the bear-shirted Norse warriors who fought in a frenzy better known?

**6   SCIENCE AND NATURE**
What is the unit of electrical resistance?

**7   LITERATURE**
Who created the literary aristocratic sleuth Lord Peter Wimsey?

**8   CELEBRITIES**
Cynthia Nixon played which professional role in the TV series *Sex and the City*?

**9   WORDS**
What are you if you are 'fubsy'?
- a) drunk
- b) stupid
- c) short

**10   POT LUCK**
'Oneiromancy' is a form of divination using what?

ANSWERS ON PAGE 292

# QUIZ 227

**1 MOVIES**
In *Citizen Kane*, what is Kane's dying word?

**2 MUSIC**
Which jazz giant recorded the albums *Sketches of Spain* and *Bitches Brew*?

**3 TV AND RADIO**
In which 1990s sitcom did Chris Barrie manage a leisure centre?

**4 SPORT AND LEISURE**
What is the Japanese sport of fencing with wooden swords called?

**5 GEOGRAPHY**
What is the capital city of Switzerland?

**6 SCIENCE AND NATURE**
What colour is the gemstone peridot, the birthstone for August?

**7 ART**
Who is famous for painting the ceiling of the Sistine Chapel in the Vatican?

**8 CELEBRITIES**
Mila Jovovich starred eponymously as which martyr in a 1999 Luc Besson film?

**9 WORDS**
What is a 'grampus'?
- a) a killer whale
- b) a woodwind instrument
- c) a sorceress

**10 POT LUCK**
What was the name of the cartoon cat determined to catch Tweety Pie?

ANSWERS ON PAGE 292

229

# QUIZ 228

**1  MOVIES**
Helen Slater starred as which comic book character in 1984?

**2  MUSIC**
Who wrote *The Mikado*?

**3  TV AND RADIO**
Elizabeth Montgomery and Dick York starred in which US sitcom?

**4  SPORT AND LEISURE**
What is the colour of the centre line in ice hockey?

**5  GEOGRAPHY**
Where is Timbuktu?

**6  SCIENCE AND NATURE**
Which disease, endemic in parts of Asia, is brought on by a deficiency of vitamin $B_1$?

**7  LITERATURE**
Who wrote *The Fall of the House of Usher*?

**8  CELEBRITIES**
Nicolas Cage is the nephew of which famous film director?

**9  WORDS**
What is a 'prolegomenon'?
  a) an introduction
  b) a prosthetic limb
  c) a mythical creature

**10  POT LUCK**
What nickname was given to New York's 28th Street, famous for popular music publishing?

ANSWERS ON PAGE 292

# QUIZ 229

**1 MOVIES**
Which early star of the talkies was originally known as Asa Yoelson?

**2 MUSIC**
'Avenues and Alleyways' and 'Is This the Way to Amarillo' were hits for which UK vocalist?

**3 TV AND RADIO**
Who played Rumpole of the Bailey?

**4 SPORT AND LEISURE**
Which British swimmer won a gold medal in the men's 100m breaststroke event in the 1980 Olympics?

**5 GEOGRAPHY**
In which country would you find the Tiber river?

**6 SCIENCE AND NATURE**
Brimstone is an obsolete name for which chemical element?

**7 LITERATURE**
Who wrote *The Secret History*?

**8 CELEBRITIES**
In which Will Smith movie did Amber Valletta play glamorous celebrity Allegra Cole?

**9 WORDS**
'Cretonne' is used in what?
- a) furnishing
- b) cooking
- c) surgery

**10 POT LUCK**
Who was the son of Daedalus, whose wings melted in the sun?

ANSWERS ON PAGE 293

# QUIZ 230

**1 MOVIES**
Who played Liv Tyler's father in 1998's *Armageddon*?

**2 MUSIC**
'Paradise City' and 'November Rain' were hits for which group?

**3 TV AND RADIO**
Which vehicles featured primarily in the 1950s TV show *Whirlybirds*?

**4 SPORT AND LEISURE**
Which cricketer reached a record of 10,123 runs in Test cricket in 1993?

**5 GEOGRAPHY**
What is the capital city of Venezuela?

**6 SCIENCE AND NATURE**
In reflexology, ailments are treated by the massage of what?

**7 ART**
Rachel Whiteread, Antony Gormley and Damien Hirst consecutively won which prize in the 1990s?

**8 CELEBRITIES**
In which sitcom do Debra Messing and Eric McCormack star?

**9 WORDS**
Something which is 'deracinated' is what?
        a) nonsensical
        b) without a roof
        c) uprooted

**10 POT LUCK**
What nationality was the composer Leos Janácek?

ANSWERS ON PAGE 293

# QUIZ 231

**1 MOVIES**
With which leading man did Deborah Kerr frolic in the surf in *From Here to Eternity*?

**2 MUSIC**
Which note is equal in time to half a minim?

**3 TV AND RADIO**
Allison Janney won an Emmy award for her role as C J Cregg in which US drama series?

**4 SPORT AND LEISURE**
Muirfield in Scotland and Royal Birkdale and the Belfry in England have been international venues in which sport?

**5 HISTORY**
Who was the only British prime minister to be assassinated?

**6 SCIENCE AND NATURE**
'Hanepoot' is a kind of which fruit?

**7 LITERATURE**
Queequeg was the Polynesian harpooner aboard which ship in *Moby Dick*?

**8 CELEBRITIES**
In which 1990s movie thriller did Robert De Niro star with Natascha McElhone and Sean Bean?

**9 WORDS**
What would you do with a 'tabla'?
- a) wear it
- b) eat it
- c) play it

**10 POT LUCK**
To which evil spirit did Faust sell his soul in German legend?

ANSWERS ON PAGE 293

# QUIZ 232

**1 MOVIES**
Claudia Cardinale starred with Henry Fonda and Charles Bronson in which 1968 western?

**2 MUSIC**
Rodrigo's *Concierto de Aranjuez* was composed for an orchestra and which solo instrument?

**3 TV AND RADIO**
Who played Remington Steele in the 1980s TV series of the same name?

**4 SPORT AND LEISURE**
'The Invincibles', who went through the 1888–89 football season undefeated, were from which English town?

**5 HISTORY**
In what year was the Wall Street crash?

**6 SCIENCE AND NATURE**
North Americans call it zucchini. How is this vegetable better known in the UK?

**7 LITERATURE**
In which Shakespeare play would you find Prospero and Caliban?

**8 CELEBRITIES**
In which US TV series did Amanda Donohoe play lawyer C J Lamb?

**9 WORDS**
An 'epilimnion' is a layer of what?
        a) water in a lake
        b) fur on a monkey
        c) chocolate in a cake

**10 POT LUCK**
In which Australian state would you find the city of Melbourne?

ANSWERS ON PAGE 293

# QUIZ 233

1 **MOVIES**
Who played the golf caddy title character in Robert Redford's movie *The Legend of Bagger Vance*?

2 **MUSIC**
Which instrument was played by Candy Dulfer on the 1990 hit single 'Lily Was Here'?

3 **TV AND RADIO**
Roy Thinnes starred as architect David Vincent in which 1960s sci-fi series?

4 **SPORT AND LEISURE**
Which team won the first American Football Super Bowl in 1967?

5 **GEOGRAPHY**
On which Scottish island is Fingal's Cave?

6 **SCIENCE AND NATURE**
Which three-headed muscle extends the forearm?

7 **LITERATURE**
Which children's character, created by Alf Prøysen, frequently shrinks uncontrollably to a height of just a few inches?

8 **CELEBRITIES**
Reese Witherspoon played Elle Woods, an unlikely student at Harvard Law School, in which 2001 movie?

9 **WORDS**
What is 'chervil'?
a) a worm infestation
b) a nautical direction
c) an aromatic plant

10 **POT LUCK**
An old warning says to cast not a clout till which month is out?

ANSWERS ON PAGE 293

# QUIZ 234

**1 MOVIES**
In which US state is the Sundance Film Festival held?

**2 MUSIC**
Which African-American singer published an autobiography called *Here I Stand* in 1958?

**3 TV AND RADIO**
Zoe Lucker played which character in *Footballers' Wives* and *Bad Girls*?

**4 SPORT AND LEISURE**
Which Frenchman was elected as president of the European footballing body UEFA in 2007?

**5 GEOGRAPHY**
In which country would you find the Paphos world heritage site?

**6 SCIENCE AND NATURE**
By which kind of creature is the disease 'psittacosis' spread?

**7 LITERATURE**
Who wrote *Angels and Demons* and *The Da Vinci Code*?

**8 CELEBRITIES**
In which 1985 Ridley Scott film did Tom Cruise star?

**9 WORDS**
What is a 'numpty'?
- a) a sizeable quantity
- b) an idiot
- c) an old-fashioned cup

**10 POT LUCK**
From which fruit is the cider-like drink perry made?

ANSWERS ON PAGE 293

# QUIZ 235

**1 MOVIES**
Dragons terrorize Britain in which 2002 movie starring Christian Bale and Alice Krige?

**2 MUSIC**
Who composed the operas *La Bohème* and *Madama Butterfly*?

**3 TV AND RADIO**
Which early Channel Five programme was a quick-fire quiz show with no visible host?

**4 SPORT AND LEISURE**
Which England football captain played for Blackpool from 1954 to 1971?

**5 GEOGRAPHY**
Of which country did General Pervez Musharraf become the president after a 1999 coup?

**6 SCIENCE AND NATURE**
How many centimetres are there in a decimetre?

**7 LITERATURE**
Who wrote the *Famous Five* and *Secret Seven* stories?

**8 CELEBRITIES**
Dannii Minogue had a UK Top Ten hit with her debut single. What was it called?

**9 WORDS**
What is 'cockeye bob' Australian slang for?
- a) a storm
- b) a sausage
- c) a sheep

**10 POT LUCK**
Which English king signed the Magna Carta?

ANSWERS ON PAGE 294

# QUIZ 236

**1 MOVIES**
In which early Tim Burton movie did Winona Ryder star with Michael Keaton and Geena Davis?

**2 MUSIC**
Who wrote *Eine Kleine Nachtmusik*?

**3 TV AND RADIO**
Chris Tarrant, Lenny Henry and Sally James hosted which anarchic ITV children's show?

**4 SPORT AND LEISURE**
Where were the Winter Olympics held in 1994?

**5 HISTORY**
Which British town was known by the Romans as Camulodunum?

**6 SCIENCE AND NATURE**
What would a 'vermivorous' animal eat?

**7 LITERATURE**
In which Thomas Hardy novel would you encounter Bathsheba Everdene?

**8 CELEBRITIES**
Which celebrity was the mother of former *Blue Peter* presenter Caron Keating?

**9 WORDS**
What is a 'palimpsest'?
> a) an architectural feature
> b) a medical treatment
> c) a manuscript

**10 POT LUCK**
Which composer wrote the music for the ballets *The Nutcracker* and *Swan Lake*?

ANSWERS ON PAGE 294

# QUIZ 237

1 **MOVIES**
Who played Dr Watson in the Basil Rathbone *Sherlock Holmes* movies?

2 **MUSIC**
Which duo wrote and performed 'The Hippopotamus Song'?

3 **TV AND RADIO**
What was the surname of Margo and Jerry in *The Good Life*?

4 **SPORT AND LEISURE**
On what sort of surface was the 18th-century game bandy played?

5 **HISTORY**
Which arm did Nelson lose?

6 **SCIENCE AND NATURE**
Coquette, hermit, racket-tail, rainbow, rubythroat, sapphire-wing and topaz are all types of which bird?

7 **LITERATURE**
Which *Fast Show* comedian has started a series of novels featuring the young James Bond?

8 **CELEBRITIES**
*Home and Away* star Melissa George appeared in a remake of which 1970s horror movie?

9 **WORDS**
If someone is 'prolix', what are they?
        a) tongue-tied
        b) dim-witted
        c) long-winded

10 **POT LUCK**
Which interior design discipline is named after the Chinese words for wind and water?

ANSWERS ON PAGE 294

# QUIZ 238

**1 MOVIES**
Which film did Francis Ford Coppola direct between *The Godfather* and *The Godfather Part II*?

**2 MUSIC**
Of which R & B group was Beyoncé a member?

**3 TV AND RADIO**
What was the name of Jane Seymour's *Medicine Woman*?

**4 SPORT AND LEISURE**
How many players are there in a shinty team?

**5 GEOGRAPHY**
Which British city is known as the 'Athens of the North'?

**6 SCIENCE AND NATURE**
In which organ of the body would you find the pineal gland?

**7 ART**
Annie Leibowitz and Mario Testino are famous in which artistic field?

**8 CELEBRITIES**
Nicole Kidman starred in a 2004 remake of which Nanette Newman movie of the 1970s?

**9 WORDS**
What is 'prestidigitation'?
        a) sleight of hand
        b) anxious gesturing
        c) quickness of hands while playing the piano

**10 POT LUCK**
In the Beatrix Potter story, what kind of animal was Samuel Whiskers?

ANSWERS ON PAGE 294

# QUIZ 239

**1  MOVIES**
The British movie *Backbeat* is a fictional portrait of which band?

**2  MUSIC**
Which progressive rock group named themselves after the inventor of the seed drill?

**3  TV AND RADIO**
Who played George Smiley in the BBC's 1970s adaptation of *Tinker, Tailor, Soldier, Spy*?

**4  SPORT AND LEISURE**
In which sport do hounds hunt game using sight rather than scent?

**5  HISTORY**
Who was the first Chairman of the People's Republic of China?

**6  SCIENCE AND NATURE**
The dodo was principally native to which island?

**7  LITERATURE**
Which Irish novelist wrote *Finnegans Wake*?

**8  CELEBRITIES**
What was the name of the character played by Billie Piper in *Doctor Who*?

**9  WORDS**
To what would you add a 'cedilla'?
    a) a fruit cake
    b) a woodwind instrument
    c) a letter of the alphabet

**10  POT LUCK**
In Irish folklore, which spirit wails and shrieks under the window of someone near death?

ANSWERS ON PAGE 294

# QUIZ 240

**1 MOVIES**
On whose stories were the films *The Shipping News* and *Brokeback Mountain* based?

**2 MUSIC**
'Freak Like Me' by the Sugababes sampled which Gary Numan song?

**3 TV AND RADIO**
Which jazz musician also presents Radio 4's *I'm Sorry I Haven't a Clue*?

**4 SPORT AND LEISURE**
Which French Formula One driver won his first Grand Prix in 1981 and was world champion four times?

**5 GEOGRAPHY**
Which Portuguese city was devastated by an earthquake in 1755?

**6 SCIENCE AND NATURE**
Apart from the Sun, which is the nearest star to the Earth?

**7 ART**
Who painted *Raft of the Medusa* in 1819?

**8 CELEBRITIES**
Which part of her body did model Caprice alter for the TV programme *Celebrities Disfigured*?

**9 WORDS**
If something is 'reticulate', what form is it in?
- a) a cord
- b) a wafer
- c) a net

**10 POT LUCK**
What was the sailor called in the Tintin stories?

ANSWERS ON PAGE 294

# QUIZ 241

**1  MOVIES**
Hitchcock's movie *Notorious* featured Ingrid Bergman with which of her *Casablanca* co-stars?

**2  MUSIC**
'Achy Breaky Heart' was a Top Ten hit in 1992 for which US singer?

**3  TV AND RADIO**
Which US TV series of the 1970s and 1980s featured a weekly array of romances aboard a cruise liner?

**4  SPORT AND LEISURE**
Which Belgian football player revolutionized the transfer market after suing the Belgian FA for restraint of trade?

**5  GEOGRAPHY**
Of which African country is Abuja the capital?

**6  SCIENCE AND NATURE**
Which scientist proposed the Gaia theory?

**7  LITERATURE**
British horror author James Herbert wrote a gory series of books about which animals?

**8  CELEBRITIES**
Who has presented *The Sky at Night* on the BBC since 1957?

**9  WORDS**
When does something 'vespertine' take place?
- a) morning
- b) evening
- c) night

**10  POT LUCK**
The 1980s film *The Name of the Rose* was based on a novel by which Italian writer?

ANSWERS ON PAGE 295

# QUIZ 242

**1 MOVIES**
Who directed *Hallowe'en*, *The Fog* and *Prince of Darkness*?

**2 MUSIC**
'No Way No Way' was a 1997 novelty single for which girl band?

**3 TV AND RADIO**
In which BBC sitcom did Altered Images singer Clare Grogan star as Kochanski?

**4 SPORT AND LEISURE**
Which Scottish racing driver was world champion in 1969, 1971 and 1973?

**5 GEOGRAPHY**
Of which Indian Ocean island is Port Louis the capital?

**6 SCIENCE AND NATURE**
What was the name of the dog that travelled on Sputnik 2?

**7 LITERATURE**
Which champion of euthanasia and author of *Darkness At Noon* committed suicide in 1983?

**8 CELEBRITIES**
Which Italian fashion designer moved into the limelight after the murder of her brother Gianni in 1997?

**9 WORDS**
'Phalanges' are what sort of bones?
       a) rib
       b) wrist
       c) finger

**10 POT LUCK**
Tagálog is the language of which island group?

ANSWERS ON PAGE 295

# QUIZ 243

**1  MOVIES**
*Bend It Like Beckham* lead Parminder Nagra went on to star in which US TV medical series?

**2  MUSIC**
Chesney Hawkes's father Len sang in which famous 1960s band?

**3  TV AND RADIO**
The Booths and the Reynolds lived next door to each other in which 1970s sitcom?

**4  SPORT AND LEISURE**
Which record-breaking motorcyclist, 26 times a TT winner, was killed in a race in Estonia in July 2000?

**5  GEOGRAPHY**
By what name did Westerners formerly know the Indian city of Mumbai?

**6  SCIENCE AND NATURE**
The 17th-century physician William Harvey is principally famous for discovering what in the human body?

**7  LITERATURE**
*The Da Vinci Code* is Dan Brown's fourth published novel. What was the title of his first?

**8  CELEBRITIES**
In which Ridley Scott movie did Eva Green star as Sibylla?

**9  WORDS**
What is a 'petiole'?
- a) an umbrella
- b) a leaf stalk
- c) an undergarment

**10  POT LUCK**
What does the French phrase 'cordon bleu' mean literally?

ANSWERS ON PAGE 295

# QUIZ 244

**1 MOVIES**
Winona Ryder starred with Dan Hedaya in which sci-fi movie sequel?

**2 MUSIC**
Which band recorded an album called *A Night at the Opera*?

**3 TV AND RADIO**
Miranda Richardson played the Queen in *Blackadder II*, but who played Lord Melchett?

**4 SPORT AND LEISURE**
What, in cycling, is a 'peloton'?

**5 GEOGRAPHY**
What is the principal language in Burkina Faso?

**6 SCIENCE AND NATURE**
Which garden bird's Latin name is *Troglodytes troglodytes*, meaning 'cave-dweller'?

**7 LITERATURE**
Which famous thriller writer, who died in 1964, had the middle name Lancaster?

**8 CELEBRITIES**
Which former wife of Andrew Lloyd Webber once sang with Hot Gossip?

**9 WORDS**
What does 'surcease' mean?
- a) to stop
- b) to make less difficult
- c) to make more expensive

**10 POT LUCK**
Which male Christian name literally means 'lover of horses'?

ANSWERS ON PAGE 295

# QUIZ 245

### 1 MOVIES
Which band's farewell concert was filmed by Martin Scorsese in 1978 as *The Last Waltz*?

### 2 MUSIC
'We are Detective', 'Doctor Doctor' and 'Hold Me Now' were hits for which 1980s band?

### 3 TV AND RADIO
On which children's TV show was Hamble the doll replaced by Poppy in 1986?

### 4 SPORT AND LEISURE
At which athletic discipline did Sergei Bubka excel?

### 5 HISTORY
Who was the British prime minister between 1964 and 1970?

### 6 SCIENCE AND NATURE
What is the collective noun for a group of ravens?

### 7 ART
Which 19th-century artist painted *The Jockey* and *At the Moulin Rouge*?

### 8 CELEBRITIES
Which character does Linda Cardellini play in the *Scooby Doo* movies?

### 9 WORDS
If something is 'loricate', what does it have?
- a) an articulated tail
- b) a hard outer coating
- c) a prominent plume

### 10 POT LUCK
Who starred as Calamity Jane in the movie of the same name?

ANSWERS ON PAGE 295

# QUIZ 246

**1 MOVIES**

Which Olympic gold medallist shot to international stardom for his role as Tarzan in twelve Hollywood movies?

**2 MUSIC**

Who sang 'I Can't Smile Without You' in 1978?

**3 TV AND RADIO**

Which popular radio programme began with the phrase 'Are you sitting comfortably? Then I'll begin'?

**4 SPORT AND LEISURE**

In darts, how many points is a bull's eye worth?

**5 GEOGRAPHY**

Which is the largest island in the Mediterranean?

**6 SCIENCE AND NATURE**

How is the constellation Ursa Major better known in English?

**7 ART**

The English painter Stanley Spencer is most closely associated with which Thames-side village?

**8 CELEBRITIES**

Actress Carrie Fisher has a famous mother. Who is she?

**9 WORDS**

What is a 'cuckold'?
- a) a type of chicken
- b) an old-fashioned kettle
- c) a man whose wife has been unfaithful

**10 POT LUCK**

The skin of which type of animal was originally used to make chamois leather?

ANSWERS ON PAGE 295

# QUIZ 247

**1   MOVIES**
Which controversial 1989 film by Peter Greenaway starred
Michael Gambon and Helen Mirren?

**2   MUSIC**
Which Brazilian singer is best known for her vocals on 'The Girl
from Ipanema'?

**3   TV AND RADIO**
Which radio and television presenter bought Virgin Radio from
Sir Richard Branson in 1997?

**4   SPORT AND LEISURE**
In which year was the first London marathon held?

**5   GEOGRAPHY**
What is the capital of Taiwan?

**6   SCIENCE AND NATURE**
How many permanent teeth does an adult have?

**7   ART**
The painting *The Madonna of the Pinks* was acquired by the
National Gallery in 2004 for £22 million. Who was the artist?

**8   CELEBRITIES**
Which chef was accompanied on many of his travels by Chalky,
his Jack Russell?

**9   WORDS**
What would be caused by 'horripilation'?
 a) goosebumps
 b) fainting
 c) sneezing

**10   POT LUCK**
How many universities are there in the USA's prestigious 'Ivy
League'?

ANSWERS ON PAGE 296

# QUIZ 248

**1   MOVIES**
Which well-known US actor was born Marion Morrison in 1907?

**2   MUSIC**
Whose single 'You Really Got Me' reached Number One in the UK singles charts in 1964?

**3   TV AND RADIO**
Which popular and long-running BBC variety show was recorded live at Leeds City Varieties, and required its audience members to dress in period costume?

**4   SPORT AND LEISURE**
Which Spanish cyclist rode to victory in five successive Tours de France from 1991 to 1995?

**5   GEOGRAPHY**
Which is the smallest country in the world?

**6   ART**
Who created the *Angel of the North*, the largest sculpture in the UK?

**7   SCIENCE AND NATURE**
From which fragrant flowering plant do we obtain vanilla?

**8   CELEBRITIES**
What nationality is the actress Salma Hayek?

**9   WORDS**
What is 'borborygmus'?
  a) the sound of distant thunder
  b) the sound of a distant train
  c) the sound of wind in one's intestines

**10   POT LUCK**
In Morse code, which letter is represented by a single dot?

ANSWERS ON PAGE 296

# QUIZ 249

**1  MOVIES**
In the Disney film *Snow White and the Seven Dwarfs*, who is the only dwarf who doesn't speak?

**2  MUSIC**
Which German composer wrote the *Goldberg Variations*?

**3  TV AND RADIO**
Which British actress won an Oscar for her role as the eponymous heroine in *The Prime of Miss Jean Brodie*?

**4  SPORT AND LEISURE**
Which Olympic sport was originally known as 'football in the water'?

**5  GEOGRAPHY**
In which country is the Muslim holy city of Mecca?

**6  SCIENCE AND NATURE**
The BCG vaccine protects against which disease?

**7  ART**
Which early modern school of art takes its name from the French word for 'wild beast'?

**8  CELEBRITIES**
Which statuesque US actress starred alongside Marilyn Monroe in *Gentlemen Prefer Blondes*?

**9  WORDS**
How would a 'filibuster' obstruct the passing of laws?
- a) by wrestling politicians
- b) by making lengthy speeches
- c) by hiding the necessary paperwork

**10  POT LUCK**
What are the main ingredients of a daiquiri cocktail?

ANSWERS ON PAGE 296

# QUIZ 250

**1 MOVIES**
Which film is known as *All Together with Passion* in Italy, *Smiles and Tears* in Spain and *The Rebel Novice* in Brazil?

**2 MUSIC**
Which composer wrote the music for the 1993 film *The Piano*?

**3 TV AND RADIO**
Who was the bowler-hatted resident of 52 Festive Road, London?

**4 SPORT AND LEISURE**
The Coupe Aéronautique Gordon Bennett is a celebrated trophy in which sport?

**5 GEOGRAPHY**
What is the name of the small principality situated in the central Pyrenees between France and Spain?

**6 SCIENCE AND NATURE**
In which year was Louise Brown, the world's first 'test-tube baby', born?

**7 ART**
In which art gallery can *Primavera* by Alessandro Botticelli be found?

**8 CELEBRITIES**
Which celebrity chef is a majority shareholder of Norwich City Football Club?

**9 WORDS**
If someone has 'Titian hair', would they be?
  a) a redhead
  b) a brunette
  c) balding

**10 POT LUCK**
The flag of which Middle Eastern country depicts a cedar tree?

ANSWERS ON PAGE 296

# SOLUTIONS

# SOLUTIONS

## QUIZ 1

1. *Thunderball*
2. the piano
3. Chigley
4. Don Bradman
5. H H Asquith
6. the Ouse
7. it does not contain the letter E
8. carbon
9. b) a literary assistant
10. in a churchyard

## QUIZ 2

1. *Dancer in the Dark*
2. drums
3. *Angels*
4. Sugar Ray
5. Albania
6. guns
7. Paddington
8. *Curb Your Enthusiasm*
9. a) beauty
10. Bob Dylan

## QUIZ 3

1. *Shakespeare in Love*
2. Mexico
3. *Countdown*
4. Fulham
5. the American Civil War
6. Ottawa
7. Paris and London
8. Buzz Aldrin
9. c) an item of clothing
10. 6 feet/1.8 metres

## QUIZ 4

1. *The Man with the Golden Gun*
2. Miles Davis
3. a dog
4. a Grand Slam
5. General Franco
6. the brain
7. Brian Clough
8. *Eternal Sunshine of the Spotless Mind*
9. a) sunlight
10. brown

## QUIZ 5

1. Sir Alec Guinness and Ewan McGregor
2. 'Wuthering Heights'
3. Sue Lawley
4. the jack
5. 1805
6. Alaska
7. *Catch 22*
8. chlorophyll
9. c) crossroads
10. the courgette

## QUIZ 6

1. Freddy Krueger
2. Suzi Quatro
3. Niles
4. Mayfair
5. Brasília
6. one
7. *Don Quixote*
8. *Mission Impossible II*
9. a) a stick for stirring porridge
10. Rex Harrison

# SOLUTIONS

## QUIZ 7
1. Jon Voight
2. Mozart
3. Prunella Scales
4. London
5. Ming
6. France
7. Phillip Pullman
8. Challenger
9. a) easily broken
10. Esperanto

## QUIZ 8
1. Bill Murray
2. Queen
3. *The X-Files*
4. golf
5. Peru
6. Marie Curie
7. Enid Blyton
8. *A for Andromeda*
9. c) greed
10. the shoulders

## QUIZ 9
1. Woody Allen
2. *Austin Powers: The Spy Who Shagged Me*
3. President of the United States
4. Jack Nicklaus
5. Peter Phillips
6. Ayers Rock
7. Margaret Thatcher
8. the Jurassic
9. c) cats
10. Vulcan

## QUIZ 10
1. *Touch of Evil*
2. *The Magic Flute*
3. *Soap*
4. Mike Gatting
5. Spiro Agnew
6. Mars
7. Tom Wolfe
8. Total Recall
9. c) a thick cloth
10. nuts

## QUIZ 11
1. *Romeo and Juliet*
2. Laurel and Hardy
3. the Green Cross Code Man
4. squash
5. the 19th century
6. Rome
7. Agatha Christie
8. amber
9. c) spiralling upwards clockwise
10. on the Moon

## QUIZ 12
1. Virginia Woolf
2. Jarvis Cocker
3. the Black Pig
4. Shergar
5. Mikhail Gorbachev
6. temperature
7. Frederick Forsyth
8. *Stranger Than Fiction*
9. b) a concubine
10. the M62

# SOLUTIONS

## QUIZ 13

1 the Maltese Falcon
2 Jonathan Creek
3 *Prisoner Cell Block H*
4 W G Grace
5 Marco Polo
6 the Caledonian Canal
7 Anne Robinson
8 17
9 c) part of a sundial
10 Arthur Miller

## QUIZ 14

1 *Se7en*
2 The Goombay Dance Band
3 Spectrum
4 Ronaldinho
5 Taiwan
6 Three Mile Island
7 *The Two Towers*
8 *The Railway Children*
9 b) of little value
10 corgi

## QUIZ 15

1 Turin
2 Limp Bizkit
3 a dog and a cat respectively
4 Arsenal
5 Henry V
6 Havana
7 Mycroft
8 the television
9 a) a self-taught person
10 Deuteronomy

## QUIZ 16

1 *Boogie Nights*
2 *Monty Python's Flying Circus*
3 Marge Simpson
4 volleyball
5 Utah
6 Austria
7 James Herriot
8 *The English Patient*
9 c) vegetables
10 the Devil

## QUIZ 17

1 Mel Gibson
2 Massive Attack
3 *The Singing Detective*
4 Virginia Wade
5 Idlewild
6 Easter Island
7 *The Day of the Triffids*
8 hydrogen
9 b) prone to using long words
10 the tongue

## QUIZ 18

1 *Rosemary's Baby*
2 Alvin Stardust
3 John Craven
4 an extra hand
5 Martin Luther King
6 purple
7 William Shakespeare
8 *Minority Report*
9 a) dark
10 the fifth

# SOLUTIONS

## QUIZ 19

1 the Ghostbusters
2 New Order
3 Derek Fowlds
4 New Zealand
5 Hannibal
6 Lithuania
7 John Galsworthy
8 the dodo
9 a) a skin treatment
10 a tumbler

## QUIZ 20

1 *Duck Soup*
2 George Frideric Handel
3 *Hart to Hart*
4 Muhammad Ali
5 Haiti
6 the head
7 Fu Manchu
8 *The Long Good Friday*
9 b) dissident literature
10 Trigger

## QUIZ 21

1 Walter Matthau
2 Jimi Hendrix
3 John Peel
4 Gordon Banks
5 the balaclava
6 Guernsey
7 Winston Churchill
8 Isaac Newton
9 bum fodder
10 *The Streets of San Francisco*

## QUIZ 22

1 *Annie Hall*
2 Ash
3 *The Water Margin*
4 2000
5 HMS *Victory*
6 rickets
7 Anton Chekhov
8 *Finding Nemo*
9 a) the proportion of light it reflects
10 three

## QUIZ 23

1 *Escape to Victory*
2 *The Young Ones*
3 Ivor the Engine
4 the Kentucky Derby
5 China
6 the Cinque Ports
7 Dame Iris Murdoch
8 Mars and Jupiter
9 b) carefully chosen
10 Theodore Roosevelt

## QUIZ 24

1 *Monster*
2 Dolly Parton
3 Daleks
4 one
5 Nepal
6 brown
7 *Valley of the Dolls*
8 John Hannah
9 b) grinding corn
10 Felix

# SOLUTIONS

## QUIZ 25

1. Cary Grant
2. Bob Dylan
3. Stan Ogden
4. Ayrton Senna
5. Harold II
6. the Faroes
7. John Milton
8. the ostrich
9. c) an authorized diplomat
10. His Master's Voice

## QUIZ 26

1. *The Game*
2. Prince
3. David Attenborough
4. the Harlem Globetrotters
5. Watergate
6. Pavlov
7. Dick Francis
8. *Shampoo*
9. a) a theatre
10. Montgolfier

## QUIZ 27

1. *Chitty Chitty Bang Bang*
2. 'The Loco-Motion'
3. 24
4. Cassius Clay
5. 1989
6. Edinburgh
7. Joanne Kathleen
8. twelve
9. b) words which begin with the same sound
10. Diana Dors

## QUIZ 28

1. *The Devil Wears Prada*
2. Billy Joel
3. *The Persuaders!*
4. ludo
5. the Magna Carta
6. semaphore
7. Claude Monet
8. *Emmerdale*
9. b) a sedimentary clay
10. *Little Britain*

## QUIZ 29

1. *Interview with the Vampire*
2. Mendelssohn
3. Jeremy Paxman
4. Stuart Pearce
5. King Arthur
6. Ethiopia
7. George Orwell
8. the ampere
9. a) a half-shadow
10. Helen of Troy

## QUIZ 30

1. *The Quiet Man*
2. Adam Ant
3. Bender
4. knitting
5. 659
6. the shoulder blade
7. Terry Pratchett
8. *Best in Show*
9. c) a water cooler
10. the ukulele

# SOLUTIONS

## QUIZ 31

1  *Speed*
2  The Pogues
3  Johnny Vegas
4  Leeds United
5  Lady Godiva
6  the Orkneys
7  *Catcher in the Rye*
8  the ear
9  c) an individual section of a fruit like a raspberry
10 Cambridge University

## QUIZ 32

1  Humphrey Bogart
2  Frank Zappa
3  *Mastermind*
4  Don Revie
5  the peso
6  marsupials
7  Louis de Bernières
8  a weather presenter
9  a) kissing
10 Shiva

## QUIZ 33

1  *The African Queen*
2  'It's Raining Men'
3  *Hill Street Blues*
4  Jimmy White
5  George III
6  the Indian Ocean
7  Enid Blyton
8  the coelacanth
9  c) someone learning the alphabet
10 Prince Andrew, the Duke of York

## QUIZ 34

1  *Splash*
2  eight
3  *That's Life*
4  gymnastics
5  Manitoba
6  lead
7  *Brighton Rock*
8  *Red Sonja*
9  b) a woman
10 foot and mouth

## QUIZ 35

1  *Elephant*
2  Motorhead
3  *Rainbow*
4  Emile Heskey
5  Neville Chamberlain
6  Calais
7  George Eliot
8  60
9  c) reading bumps on the head
10 Dana Scully

## QUIZ 36

1  Gael García Bernal
2  Lionel Richie
3  *Spitting Image*
4  archery
5  the Brinks Mat robbery
6  penguin
7  *Perfume*
8  Peter Sellers
9  a) a medieval instrument
10 Daedalus

# SOLUTIONS

## QUIZ 37

1  Morgan Freeman
2  Muddy Waters
3  Dave Lee Travis
4  downhill skiing
5  Milhous
6  Anchorage
7  Rudyard Kipling
8  hydrogen and oxygen
9  b) the French word for lightning
10 grappa

## QUIZ 38

1  *Anna Karenina*
2  Barcelona
3  Adrian Mole
4  Padraig Harrington
5  Mahatma Gandhi
6  the pancreas
7  Mickey Spillane
8  *One Hour Photo*
9  c) slower
10 brigadier

## QUIZ 39

1  *Captain Corelli's Mandolin*
2  Mozart
3  Brian
4  Olga Korbut
5  Nero
6  the Sahara Desert
7  Virginia Andrews
8  tin
9  a) the study of fingerprints
10 lederhosen

## QUIZ 40

1  *The Last of the Mohicans*
2  Bob Hope
3  James Garner
4  table tennis/ping pong
5  Madagascar
6  Disk-Operating System
7  Mark Twain
8  Terry Wogan
9  c) leather
10 Germany

## QUIZ 41

1  *Passenger 57*
2  The Beach Boys
3  Ardal O'Hanlon
4  ice hockey
5  John Wilkes Booth
6  Bath
7  Richmal Crompton
8  the duodenum
9  b) an unnecessary word
10 whisky

## QUIZ 42

1  *Secretary*
2  Henry Mancini
3  *Bonanza*
4  Sugar Ray Robinson
5  Hong Kong
6  Chuck Yeager
7  *The Godfather*
8  *The Bold and the Beautiful*
9  a) a Chinese dress
10 Typhoid Mary

# SOLUTIONS

## QUIZ 43

1 *E.T. The Extra-Terrestrial*
2 The Band
3 Roy Walker
4 Len Hutton
5 Jamaica
6 Rio de Janeiro
7 Ellery Queen
8 the Sun
9 a) a conjuror
10 ballet

## QUIZ 44

1 *Ocean's Twelve*
2 The Rolling Stones
3 *The New Avengers*
4 snooker
5 Belarus
6 Frank Whittle
7 Robert Browning
8 *Inside Man*
9 b) sweet
10 the Bridge of Sighs

## QUIZ 45

1 Charlie Chaplin
2 *Graceland*
3 *Dixon of Dock Green*
4 Johnny Weissmuller
5 Catherine Parr
6 fjords
7 Bernard Cornwell
8 cloud
9 c) like a child
10 Glasgow

## QUIZ 46

1 *Dune*
2 Saint-Saëns
3 Robert Lindsay
4 James Cracknell
5 Africa
6 Albert Einstein
7 Eugene O'Neill
8 *Friends*
9 a) slugs
10 a full house

## QUIZ 47

1 Guy Pearce
2 Gilbert and Sullivan
3 *Home and Away*
4 Jock Stein
5 Idi Amin
6 the Suez Canal
7 Jane Austen
8 Mars
9 c) pearly
10 *Play School*

## QUIZ 48

1 *Private Benjamin*
2 Squeeze
3 *Sesame Street*
4 Jesse Owens
5 Terry Waite
6 the eye
7 Samuel Pepys
8 *The Talented Mr Ripley*
9 c) a bird
10 Hebrew

# SOLUTIONS

## QUIZ 49

1 *Breakfast at Tiffany's*
2 U2
3 *Albion Market*
4 American football
5 Barbara Castle
6 national parks
7 J D Salinger
8 the speed of light (in a vacuum)
9 b) a shield
10 14 July

## QUIZ 50

1 *The Fly*
2 Verdi
3 *Lost*
4 shinty
5 Boudicca
6 DNA
7 Biggles
8 *The Break-up*
9 b) an overhead transport system
10 Dario Fo

## QUIZ 51

1 *Gosford Park*
2 Shaun Ryder
3 *Come Dancing*
4 every two years
5 Poland
6 Dogger
7 Nicholas Evans
8 mercury
9 a) an extinct zebra-like animal
10 the dragon

## QUIZ 52

1 *Blue Velvet*
2 Ken Dodd
3 Robin Day
4 basketball
5 Charles Lindbergh
6 the stethoscope
7 Victor Hugo
8 *Dick Tracy*
9 a) a seaweed
10 the Crimean War

## QUIZ 53

1 *Good Will Hunting*
2 Tammy Wynette
3 *The Fall Guy*
4 Uruguay
5 Oliver Cromwell
6 San Francisco
7 Phillip Pullman
8 acid
9 c) yo-yo
10 on your head

## QUIZ 54

1 *Calamity Jane*
2 Brian May
3 *Edge of Darkness*
4 Italy
5 Benito Mussolini
6 wind
7 a Russian submarine
8 *Mr & Mrs Smith*
9 b) water
10 Vietnam

# SOLUTIONS

## QUIZ 55

1  *Betty Blue*
2  Robert Johnson
3  *Telly Addicts*
4  the Isle of Man
5  Japan
6  Greenwich
7  Alan Titchmarsh
8  Marie Curie
9  b) transparent
10 Taurus

## QUIZ 56

1  *Annie Hall*
2  Cliff Richard
3  *The Mighty Boosh*
4  Rubin Carter
5  Mauritania
6  iron
7  William Blake
8  *Boys Don't Cry*
9  a) his wife
10 ants

## QUIZ 57

1  Woody
2  Janet Ellis
3  *Vision On*
4  Eric Bristow
5  1980
6  Rwanda
7  *Trainspotting*
8  zinc
9  c) wormlike
10 red

## QUIZ 58

1  *Rebel Without a Cause*
2  Johann Sebastian Bach
3  Sam Mitchell
4  16
5  Juliana
6  Windscale
7  the Saint
8  Terry Yorath
9  b) in the depths of the ocean
10 T S Eliot

## QUIZ 59

1  *Prizzi's Honor*
2  the radio star
3  James Garner
4  surfing
5  1982
6  Sicily
7  Jeffrey Archer
8  fool's gold
9  b) deep and resonant
10 juniper

## QUIZ 60

1  Lois Lane
2  'Woman'
3  Magnum
4  Italy
5  the Bering Strait
6  the aurora australis
7  Vincent Van Gogh
8  a pot-bellied pig
9  a) a net bag
10 Robben Island

# SOLUTIONS

## QUIZ 61

1 Humphrey Bogart
2 *The Lone Ranger*
3 Syd and Eddie
4 the Super Bowl
5 Clement Attlee
6 Kentucky
7 Ben Elton
8 Ag
9 a) 100 zeros
10 Terry Venables

## QUIZ 62

1 *The Blues Brothers*
2 Lonnie Donegan
3 The Clangers
4 golf
5 Hirohito
6 swan
7 James Hogg
8 Roger Vadim
9 b) on a sword handle
10 the Oval

## QUIZ 63

1 *Fantastic Voyage*
2 Paul McCartney
3 two
4 Vijay Singh
5 Edward I
6 Burma
7 C S Lewis
8 the Sun
9 b) whales
10 David Icke

## QUIZ 64

1 Terence Stamp
2 Bros
3 *Colditz*
4 Tony Jacklin
5 Spain
6 France
7 *Fahrenheit 451*
8 Princess Anne
9 c) a South American rodent
10 the Styx

## QUIZ 65

1 *Fight Club*
2 Eric Clapton
3 David Jason
4 judo
5 the 1930s
6 Haiti
7 Dostoevsky
8 chemistry
9 a) an important man
10 Phil Lynot

## QUIZ 66

1 *Wicked Lady*
2 1988
3 William G Stewart
4 Jonny Wilkinson
5 the statue of Zeus at Olympia
6 vitamin A
7 Rex Stout
8 violin
9 a) a heavy cloth
10 Bucket

# SOLUTIONS

## QUIZ 67

1 *The Time Machine*
2 Ludwig
3 Tommy Cooper
4 the Crucible Theatre
5 Harry S Truman
6 K2
7 *Midnight's Children*
8 iron
9 c) colossal
10 Hinduism

## QUIZ 68

1 *Flushed Away*
2 Serge Gainsbourg
3 *The Shield*
4 The Netherlands
5 William IV
6 platypus
7 Isaac Asimov
8 *Giant*
9 a) trees
10 Alexander the Great

## QUIZ 69

1 *Lawrence of Arabia*
2 Herbie Hancock
3 *Sapphire and Steel*
4 the caber
5 Rudolph Giuliani
6 the Mediterranean Sea
7 Peter Benchley
8 the kilobyte
9 c) a Turkish infantryman
10 Hungarian

## QUIZ 70

1 Charles Laughton
2 Leeds
3 Ian Richardson
4 Björn Borg
5 China
6 a swan
7 *Vanity Fair*
8 Pamela Anderson
9 b) criticize
10 Switzerland

## QUIZ 71

1 *The Wicker Man*
2 Del Shannon
3 Nicholas Parsons
4 Clive Lloyd
5 1789
6 Philadelphia
7 Arthur C Clarke
8 Isambard Kingdom Brunel
9 a) the curved surface of a liquid
10 the elephant

## QUIZ 72

1 *Mona Lisa Smile*
2 'Unforgettable'
3 Kevin McCloud
4 Colin McRae
5 the Black Panthers
6 lanthanum
7 Branwell
8 *ER*
9 a) an ear
10 Spain

# SOLUTIONS

## QUIZ 73

1  Laura Palmer
2  Joan Jett and the Blackhearts
3  *Butterflies*
4  Sir Bobby Robson
5  Edward VII
6  Barbados
7  Michael Moore
8  light-emitting diode
9  belladonna
10  a) 7,900

## QUIZ 74

1  *Natural Born Killers*
2  trumpet
3  Bamber Gascoigne
4  bobsleigh
5  'La Marseillaise'
6  the tog-value
7  Haruki Murakami
8  John Malkovich
9  b) a werewolf
10  the 15th

## QUIZ 75

1  *The Shining*
2  Spandau Ballet
3  *Charlie's Angels*
4  Vijay Amritraj
5  Leonard Spencer
6  Antipodes
7  *Doctor Zhivago*
8  the fulmar
9  c) rhubarb
10  A3

## QUIZ 76

1  *Empire of the Sun*
2  Earth Wind and Fire
3  Jimmy Tarbuck
4  Sally Gunnell
5  Henry II
6  the atomic bomb
7  *Rebecca*
8  *Tomorrow's World*
9  c) weaken them
10  the calliope

## QUIZ 77

1  James Stewart
2  with increasing speed
3  Sir Alan Sugar
4  Sonny Liston
5  Gary Powers
6  the Zambezi
7  Reginald Hill
8  Hale–Bopp
9  a) poodle
10  *Romeo and Juliet*

## QUIZ 78

1  Keira Knightley
2  the theremin
3  *Blake's 7*
4  Le Mans 24-Hour
5  Helen Sharman
6  soap
7  Ernest Hemingway
8  Johnny Depp
9  c) flags
10  *The Transformers*

# SOLUTIONS

## QUIZ 79

1. none
2. Showaddywaddy
3. *Blue Peter*
4. 1967
5. Walter Sickert
6. Tasmania
7. Len Deighton
8. eleven years
9. a) torpedo
10. a seed drill

## QUIZ 80

1. Gilbert and Sullivan
2. Benny Hill
3. *Boys from the Blackstuff*
4. Steve Ovett
5. Italy
6. Pluto
7. Dashiell Hammett
8. telescope
9. b) sleight of hand
10. Harry Houdini

## QUIZ 81

1. *The Matrix*
2. Billie Holiday
3. Sage
4. darts
5. the Byzantine Empire
6. Hungary
7. Edgar Rice Burroughs
8. they grow up
9. a) a window
10. Boris Johnson

## QUIZ 82

1. Tommy Lee Jones
2. 'Concrete and Clay'
3. Tom Barnaby
4. Hansie Cronje
5. Carthage
6. four
7. Endeavour
8. Ron Howard
9. c) sycophantic
10. ten dollars

## QUIZ 83

1. Ed Wood
2. Franz Schubert
3. *Blackadder II*
4. table tennis
5. Rudolf Hess
6. The Bahamas
7. *Gone with the Wind*
8. Joseph Priestley
9. b) a bird
10. Israel

## QUIZ 84

1. Bonnie and Clyde
2. Bill Wyman
3. *The Man from Atlantis*
4. Salt Lake City
5. twelve
6. hyena
7. Jacqueline Wilson
8. Vernon Kay
9. a) a form of torture
10. a pint

# SOLUTIONS

## QUIZ 85

1 Hammer
2 Bob Dylan
3 *How Clean is Your House?*
4 147
5 the Peasants' Revolt
6 Greenland
7 Kylie Minogue
8 the skull
9 c) a squint
10 triangular

## QUIZ 86

1 *Never Say Never Again*
2 Ultravox
3 £250,000
4 1967
5 the Gunpowder Plot
6 the eyeball
7 G K Chesterton
8 *Alfie*
9 a) a saddle pad
10 Sir Walter Scott

## QUIZ 87

1 Sean Connery
2 Rednex
3 Jeremy Clarkson
4 Jimmy Connors
5 the Hundred Years' War
6 Borneo
7 Alexandre Dumas
8 butterfly
9 salt
10 Bacchus

## QUIZ 88

1 *To Catch a Thief*
2 'I Feel Love'
3 *Trumpton*
4 Hockenheim
5 Donald Dewar
6 hydrogen
7 Billy Bunter
8 *Monster*
9 a) weak
10 anti-clockwise

## QUIZ 89

1 *The Deep*
2 Number 6 in F major
3 *Taxi*
4 Lance Armstrong
5 Indira Gandhi
6 The Netherlands
7 Billy Connolly
8 Orville and Wilbur
9 c) the nose
10 Sing Sing

## QUIZ 90

1 *Who Framed Roger Rabbit?*
2 Marshall Mathers
3 Patricia Routledge
4 golf
5 Pakistan
6 tin
7 Lewis Carroll
8 *Austin Powers in Goldmember*
9 b) a confused noise
10 a library

# SOLUTIONS

## QUIZ 91

1   *The Rock*
2   the Flaming Lips
3   Loyd Grossman
4   dive
5   the 19th century
6   three hours
7   Nicci French
8   three
9   c) a hotchpotch
10  Julian

## QUIZ 92

1   *Bad Boys*
2   'Kiss Kiss'
3   Gowen
4   Jonah Lomu
5   Denmark
6   the wild pansy
7   Roy Lichtenstein
8   Elizabeth I
9   c) marble
10  Grand Old Man

## QUIZ 93

1   John Sturges
2   Tight Fit
3   Jasper Carrott
4   the discus
5   T E Lawrence
6   Kathmandu
7   John Buchan
8   13
9   b) the underworld
10  *Private Eye*

## QUIZ 94

1   *Tristram Shandy*
2   'Sound of the Underground'
3   Ironside
4   Epsom Downs
5   Germany
6   Mexico and the USA
7   photography
8   Steve Martin
9   c) a drunken reveller
10  *Macbeth*

## QUIZ 95

1   the *Airport* series
2   Hit Me with Your Rhythm Stick'
3   Penelope Keith
4   1969
5   Iceland
6   Mozambique
7   Graham Greene
8   the hovercraft
9   b) Swedish
10  Vietnam

## QUIZ 96

1   *The Horse Whisperer*
2   the Wombles
3   a dog
4   four
5   the Macdonalds
6   fossils
7   Lewis Carroll
8   poker
9   a) a magician
10  Atlas

# SOLUTIONS

## QUIZ 97
1 Jodie Foster
2 Cher
3 Radio 1
4 Mick McCarthy
5 Egyptian
6 Arabic
7 Jean M Auel
8 19th
9 b) paper tiger
10 Flash Gordon

## QUIZ 98
1 Jason Bourne
2 Georgia
3 Ian Lavender
4 E
5 6 June
6 Neptune
7 Sylvia Plath
8 *Harry Potter and the Goblet of Fire*
9 c) wood
10 Joe DiMaggio

## QUIZ 99
1 Harrison Ford
2 Fleetwood Mac
3 Tribbiani
4 Gary Sobers
5 Paul Revere
6 North Korea
7 George Orwell
8 Michael Faraday
9 a) whipping
10 violin

## QUIZ 100
1 Barbarella
2 Rod Stewart
3 *Who Wants to Be a Millionaire*
4 tack
5 the Battle of Little Bighorn
6 Cancer
7 Arthur Conan Doyle
8 *Strictly Come Dancing*
9 b) 20
10 Hadrian's Wall

## QUIZ 101
1 Quentin Tarantino
2 'Deck of Cards'
3 *Midnight Caller*
4 Jack Brabham
5 the Alamo
6 paise
7 Harper Lee
8 lightning
9 a) to take or destroy 10 per cent of
10 Switzerland

## QUIZ 102
1 *Tomorrow Never Dies*
2 Moby
3 *NYPD Blue*
4 Bernhard Langer
5 Sri Lanka
6 laser
7 John Keats
8 *Doom*
9 b) a mathematical term
10 garnet

# SOLUTIONS

## QUIZ 103

1  *One Million Years BC*
2  *The Banana Splits*
3  Ron Pickering
4  Babe Ruth
5  the Huns
6  Chile
7  Anne
8  206
9  c) a weapon
10 Switzerland

## QUIZ 104

1  *Frenzy*
2  The Rembrandts
3  Raquel
4  Henry Cooper
5  the Roman Empire
6  vinegar
7  Tarka
8  Catwoman
9  b) a figure of speech
10 Beethoven

## QUIZ 105

1  Adolf Hitler
2  Sigue Sigue Sputnik
3  Beth Jordache
4  Stephen Hendry
5  Jimmy Carter
6  Italy
7  Vladimir Nabokov
8  John Dunlop
9  a) raspberries
10 Alfred Hitchcock

## QUIZ 106

1  *Key Largo*
2  Ugly Kid Joe
3  James Garner
4  Denmark
5  Owen Glendower
6  aspirin
7  Jeeves
8  *The Libertine*
9  b) a lion
10 20

## QUIZ 107

1  *Prizzi's Honor*
2  'Amazing Grace'
3  Hale and Pace
4  Martina Hingis
5  1948
6  Belarus
7  Madrid
8  the foxglove
9  c) servile
10 guns

## QUIZ 108

1  *The Hustler*
2  'Dirrty'
3  *The Good Old Days*
4  rugby union
5  Abraham Lincoln
6  China
7  Laura Ingalls Wilder
8  David Beckham
9  c) pregnant
10 James Callaghan

# SOLUTIONS

## QUIZ 109

1. *Network*
2. the Stone Roses
3. HMP Slade
4. West Bromwich Albion
5. Augusto Pinochet
6. Malawi
7. *The God of Small Things*
8. hooves
9. b) a domed roof
10. Vesuvius

## QUIZ 110

1. *Flightplan*
2. Liverpool
3. Orla
4. Eric Cantona
5. Shetland
6. 32°
7. *Sense and Sensibility*
8. King Kong
9. b) sleep-talking
10. the goat

## QUIZ 111

1. Kevin Kline
2. Emmylou Harris
3. Terry McCann
4. Kenny Dalglish
5. Elba
6. the Isle of Man
7. Marian Keyes
8. Daniel Fahrenheit
9. b) a saint
10. avocado

## QUIZ 112

1. *The Constant Gardener*
2. the Red Hot Chili Peppers
3. Arthur Mullard
4. Derby County
5. Hawaii
6. the badger
7. *Shane*
8. Zorro
9. c) die
10. Queen Victoria

## QUIZ 113

1. Al Pacino
2. 'Cornflake Girl'
3. Irene Handl
4. horse racing
5. Entebbe
6. the Atlantic Ocean
7. *All Quiet on the Western Front*
8. the blue whale
9. a) an ornamented gem
10. Dylan Thomas

## QUIZ 114

1. *Flatliners*
2. very quickly
3. *The A-Team*
4. an eagle
5. Israel
6. hydrogen
7. Vincent Van Gogh
8. America Ferrera
9. b) to put on oath
10. Sirius

# SOLUTIONS

## QUIZ 115

1 *Unforgiven*
2 Norway
3 *Never Mind the Buzzcocks*
4 contract bridge
5 Yuri Gagarin
6 the Caspian Sea
7 *Watership Down*
8 the apple
9 b) husband
10 30 November

## QUIZ 116

1 *The Medusa Touch*
2 Shamen
3 Alan Bennett
4 Jake La Motta
5 Franklin D Roosevelt
6 90
7 Armistead Maupin
8 Seal
9 b) a scruffy person
10 elephant

## QUIZ 117

1 *A Beautiful Mind*
2 Jive Bunny and the Mastermixers
3 *Falcon Crest*
4 Imran Khan
5 Elizabeth I
6 Finland
7 H P Lovecraft
8 Venus
9 c) preaching
10 Admiral of the Fleet

## QUIZ 118

1 New Zealand
2 The Vengaboys
3 Rick Wakeman
4 Barry Sheene
5 the Gregorian
6 Bhopal
7 Harold Pinter
8 Tony Curtis
9 c) a stone
10 she poisoned herself

## QUIZ 119

1 *The Usual Suspects*
2 'My Heart Will Go On'
3 CJ
4 Joe DiMaggio
5 the American Civil War
6 Alberta
7 *A Tale of Two Cities*
8 Sir Barnes Wallis
9 b) the rich
10 1945

## QUIZ 120

1 *Conan the Barbarian*
2 Louis Armstrong
3 Xena
4 the Republic of Ireland
5 the Trent
6 ruby
7 *Bravo Two Zero*
8 Mark Bosnich
9 b) naive
10 five gold rings

# SOLUTIONS

## QUIZ 121

1 Lon Chaney Jr
2 Handel
3 Wonder Woman
4 South Africa
5 Nelson Mandela
6 Henry Cavendish
7 Baloo
8 *Moulin Rouge*
9 a) the countryside
10 Captain Cook

## QUIZ 122

1 *Straw Dogs*
2 Tears for Fears
3 John Steed
4 American football
5 William the Conqueror
6 the skin
7 Ian Rankin
8 Snoop Dogg
9 c) modest
10 tombola

## QUIZ 123

1 *Freaks*
2 Sir Elton John
3 Jerry Springer
4 baseball or softball
5 1917
6 tungsten
7 Kevin
8 *The Brothers Grimm*
9 c) a canoe
10 the Monkees

## QUIZ 124

1 *Girl*
2 Rolf Harris
3 Richard Beckinsale
4 bantamweight
5 Bannockburn
6 the rose of Jericho
7 Anthony Trollope
8 the Osbournes
9 a) animal entrails
10 hammer and sickle

## QUIZ 125

1 God
2 Charlie Parker
3 *UFO*
4 1954
5 John Adams
6 Zimbabwe
7 Anthony Burgess
8 acidity
9 a) thick skin
10 quisling

## QUIZ 126

1 *Brazil*
2 'Baby One More Time'
3 cricket
4 James Hunt
5 *Fram*
6 Italy
7 Douglas Adams
8 long-sightedness
9 c) blancmange
10 Lady Emma Hamilton

# SOLUTIONS

## QUIZ 127

1 *American Beauty*
2 Art Garfunkel
3 Prince Charles
4 Will Carling
5 Ruth Ellis
6 ice
7 Jackson Pollock
8 *Fight Club*
9 a) blowing glass
10 ocean trenches

## QUIZ 128

1 *Cold Mountain*
2 Racey
3 *Mork and Mindy*
4 five
5 Burma
6 the mosquito
7 the *Mona Lisa*
8 Annette Crosbie
9 b) a sheep
10 a cucumber

## QUIZ 129

1 Patricia Highsmith
2 'Eleanor Rigby'
3 Martin Clunes
4 Jesse Owens
5 John
6 Mull
7 *Gone with the Wind*
8 the heart
9 b) destiny
10 an eye

## QUIZ 130

1 *Castaway*
2 19
3 *Edge of Darkness*
4 Ally MacLeod
5 Bede
6 a cat
7 *David Copperfield*
8 John Travolta
9 a) a pout
10 Jezebel

## QUIZ 131

1 Terence Stamp
2 the bagpipe
3 *South Park*
4 the Tour de France
5 the Shetland Islands
6 bees
7 Evelyn Waugh
8 Canada
9 b) a carriage
10 £25

## QUIZ 132

1 Jude Law
2 Deee-Lite
3 Jon Snow
4 Jimmy Connors
5 George V
6 Indonesia
7 Samuel Pepys
8 Charles Darwin
9 b) horse
10 United Nations Educational Scientific and Cultural Organization

# SOLUTIONS

## QUIZ 133

1 Martin Scorsese
2 Acker Bilk
3 Denise
4 Steve Ovett
5 Alexander the Great
6 Pythagoras
7 Harriet Beecher Stowe
8 Dominic Monaghan
9 c) a fox
10 Amen Corner

## QUIZ 134

1 *Dr No*
2 Hot Chocolate
3 *Ever Decreasing Circles*
4 Zola Budd
5 Slovenia
6 gunpowder
7 Christopher Marlowe
8 Goldie Hawn
9 a) overlap planks
10 the Statue of Liberty

## QUIZ 135

1 James Cameron
2 nine
3 Huggy Bear
4 Eusebio
5 Constantine II
6 Spain and France
7 Joanne Harris
8 the dinosaur
9 c) an opossum
10 Fleet Street

## QUIZ 136

1 Robert De Niro
2 Herbie Hancock
3 *The Champions*
4 Marvin Hagler
5 the *Santa Maria*
6 the computer
7 *Total Recall*
8 William
9 Sind
10 Lloyd's

## QUIZ 137

1 *The Truman Show*
2 Captain and Tennille
3 Dick Sargent
4 Tiger Woods
5 SPQR
6 Jupiter
7 C S Forester
8 *xXx*
9 b) film
10 Sabrina

## QUIZ 138

1 *Double Indemnity*
2 Deacon Blue
3 James Gandolfini
4 Pelé
5 Australia
6 Botswana
7 Charlotte
8 the atom
9 b) make it worse
10 Radiohead

# SOLUTIONS

## QUIZ 139

1. Alan Smithee
2. *Miami Vice*
3. Melanie Healy
4. Matt Le Tissier
5. Rousseau
6. minus one
7. John Wyndham
8. Jodie Foster
9. c) a curved architectural moulding
10. November

## QUIZ 140

1. *Snow White and the Seven Dwarfs*
2. *The Sopranos*
3. *Sale of the Century*
4. Bill Werbeniuk
5. Canada
6. five
7. Edvard Munch
8. Katie Price
9. c) divine
10. a flag

## QUIZ 141

1. Laurence Olivier
2. Catatonia
3. *Due South*
4. Everton
5. Mahatma
6. Rhode Island
7. Beatrix Potter
8. a machine gun
9. c) frugal
10. Chicago

## QUIZ 142

1. Virginia Woolf
2. Saint-Saëns
3. spaghetti
4. Jennifer Capriati
5. Queen Anne
6. the poppy
7. *The Bridges of Madison County*
8. L L Cool J
9. a) covetousness
10. hair

## QUIZ 143

1. *In The Cut*
2. New Zealand
3. *The Young Ones*
4. Rubin 'Hurricane' Carter
5. *Braer*
6. Iceland
7. H G Wells
8. Tracy Barlow
9. c) buried alive
10. one's dignity

## QUIZ 144

1. *Apocalypse Now*
2. Phil Spector
3. *Top Gear*
4. Magic
5. Sir Walter Raleigh
6. Mesopotamia
7. D H Lawrence
8. pain
9. b) disuse
10. Tom Waits

# SOLUTIONS

## QUIZ 145
1  *Carry On Sergeant*
2  Howard Jones
3  Peter Davison
4  Seoul, 1988
5  Franklin D Roosevelt
6  pewter
7  *Around the World in 80 Days*
8  *Training Day*
9  a) finches
10 ERNIE

## QUIZ 146
1  *Medicine Man*
2  Wet Wet Wet
3  Dennis Weaver
4  Real Madrid
5  the Bourse
6  60
7  Kurt Vonnegut
8  *Jagged Little Pill*
9  b) glittering
10 the polka

## QUIZ 147
1  Meryl Streep
2  Tchaikovsky
3  Michael Brandon
4  John Francome
5  Copernicus
6  Italy
7  Truman Capote
8  Sputnik
9  c) humidity
10 the pomegranate

## QUIZ 148
1  Woody Harrelson
2  Nick Berry
3  Robert Mitchum
4  King George VI
5  New Zealand
6  vitamin C
7  Voltaire
8  *Sky Captain and the World of Tomorrow*
9  c) pus
10 Easter

## QUIZ 149
1  Jamie Foxx
2  Chubby Checker
3  Beryl Reid
4  sumo wrestling
5  Canada
6  steel
7  St Petersburg
8  *Cruel Intentions*
9  a) a piece of climbing equipment
10 on a ship

## QUIZ 150
1  *The Birds*
2  *High Noon*
3  Cliff Barnes
4  Le Mans
5  Parliament
6  Sweden
7  Ruth Rendell
8  two
9  c) sounds like what it describes
10 the hedgehog

# SOLUTIONS

## QUIZ 151

1 *De-Lovely*
2 Babylon Zoo
3 *The Archers*
4 Dublin
5 1939
6 the narwhal
7 J M Coetzee
8 *Quadrophenia*
9 b) childbirth
10 Hamelin

## QUIZ 152

1 Ben Stiller
2 John Inman
3 David Copperfield
4 Gheorghe Hagi
5 the South Sea Bubble
6 Louis Pasteur
7 Sir John Betjeman
8 architecture
9 c) the female side of a family
10 the Keystone Cops

## QUIZ 153

1 a diamond
2 *The Man with the Golden Gun*
3 Brian Tilsley
4 Liz McColgan
5 the Wars of the Roses
6 Canberra
7 Zadie Smith
8 A
9 a) to whisper
10 Jason

## QUIZ 154

1 Val Kilmer
2 Lonnie Donegan
3 Ian Richardson
4 Paula Radcliffe
5 Finisterre
6 electric current
7 Jane Tennison
8 *Grosse Pointe Blank*
9 a) on a toadstool
10 the Bank of England

## QUIZ 155

1 *When Harry Met Sally*
2 The Bluebells
3 Scott Bakula
4 Croatian
5 Norway
6 gorillas
7 Gormenghast
8 *Cheers*
9 a) darken
10 *Lady Chatterley's Lover*

## QUIZ 156

1 alcoholism
2 Gustav
3 Bristol
4 Dame Tanni Grey-Thompson
5 Egypt
6 hyena
7 *Catch 22*
8 *Bride and Prejudice*
9 b) haphazard
10 a swastika

# SOLUTIONS

## QUIZ 157

1 Paul Newman
2 Stevie Wonder
3 *Blake's 7*
4 Diego
5 Queen Victoria
6 New Mexico
7 Martin Amis
8 cats
9 a) a drinking party
10 karaoke

## QUIZ 158

1 *Look Who's Talking*
2 Simple Minds
3 Robert Carlyle
4 Gordon Banks
5 Havana
6 the kidneys
7 Kenneth Grahame
8 Katharine Hepburn
9 a) weird
10 the 15th

## QUIZ 159

1 *Monster*
2 Pulp
3 Casey Jones
4 the USA and Europe
5 none
6 Chicago
7 Marcel Proust
8 citric acid
9 c) a funeral
10 smoking

## QUIZ 160

1 *Ladyhawke*
2 Freddie Mercury
3 a dolphin
4 Fabrizio Ravanelli
5 St David
6 the lung
7 Sir Christopher Wren
8 *National Treasure*
9 c) a bird
10 mah-jong

## QUIZ 161

1 Frank Sinatra
2 The Moody Blues
3 TV-am
4 San Francisco
5 Golda Meir
6 Mongolia
7 Stephen King
8 pressure
9 a) to disconcert
10 South Africa

## QUIZ 162

1 *Orca: The Killer Whale*
2 Jelly Roll Morton
3 Quimby
4 North America
5 Nostradamus
6 Alfred Nobel
7 Arthur Conan Doyle
8 *Dodgeball*
9 a) a meal
10 Coco Chanel

# SOLUTIONS

## QUIZ 163

1 Dooley Wilson
2 'Super Trouper' and 'The Winner Takes It All'
3 Annie Sugden
4 Prince Naseem Hamed
5 James K Polk
6 Asia
7 Charles Kingsley
8 Sir Humphry Davy
9 c) a customs official
10 Anubis

## QUIZ 164

1 *Shine*
2 The Sugarcubes
3 Rodney Bewes
4 Chicago White Sox
5 Russia
6 the swede
7 Mickey Spillane
8 nightclubs
9 b) assists learning
10 Yggdrasil

## QUIZ 165

1 *La dolce vita*
2 Number 6
3 Erik Estrada
4 Rugby Union
5 Andrei Gromyko
6 Monaco
7 Winston Churchill
8 a bat
9 b) the biblical flood
10 the eighth

## QUIZ 166

1 *Henry V*
2 Peters and Lee
3 Aled Jones
4 Greg Chappell
5 The Franks
6 green monkey disease
7 Ewan McGregor
8 USS Voyager
9 c) a logger
10 a peacock

## QUIZ 167

1 *Dog Day Afternoon*
2 *Every Which Way But Loose*
3 *Star Trek VI: The Undiscovered Country*
4 El Cordobés
5 2002
6 South Africa
7 *Macbeth*
8 Ariane
9 a) a private language
10 Sagittarius

## QUIZ 168

1 Nicolas Cage
2 *Lady and the Tramp*
3 Gareth Hunt
4 the Wimbledon tennis championships
5 France
6 coffee
7 Spanish
8 *Mystery Men*
9 a) snuff
10 Hercules/Heracles

# SOLUTIONS

## QUIZ 169

1. *Shrek*
2. Manhattan Transfer
3. Professor Yaffle
4. Derby County
5. Nike
6. Chile
7. J R R Tolkien
8. BASIC
9. c) a pea
10. Aberdeen

## QUIZ 170

1. *The Others*
2. Holly Johnson
3. *3-2-1*
4. horses
5. 1997
6. hippopotamus
7. Jerome K Jerome
8. Bob Geldof
9. a) an architectural feature
10. Hank Marvin

## QUIZ 171

1. Martin Amis
2. Coolio
3. *The Hit Man and Her*
4. golf
5. Johannes Gutenberg
6. the Hebrides
7. Bram Stoker
8. the *Amoco Cadiz*
9. a) a skating manoeuvre
10. Spain

## QUIZ 172

1. Tobey Maguire
2. The White Stripes
3. Michael Parkinson
4. 28
5. the Cinque Ports
6. the Jurassic
7. Pablo Picasso
8. Bruce Forsyth
9. a) glowing red
10. Burgundy

## QUIZ 173

1. *Guys And Dolls*
2. Jean Sibelius
3. *Love Hurts*
4. Belgian
5. 1967
6. Mongolia
7. Seabiscuit
8. stars
9. a) to outline
10. Echo

## QUIZ 174

1. *King Lear*
2. Wagner
3. *LA Law*
4. teddy bears
5. Tsar
6. DNA fingerprinting
7. Fu-Manchu
8. *Sirens*
9. b) a means of transport and leisure
10. *Sanditon*

# SOLUTIONS

## QUIZ 175

1 *Judge Dredd*
2 Mud
3 *ER*
4 a greyhound
5 Mother Theresa
6 Ethiopia
7 Michael Crichton
8 the pancreas
9 c) an arrangement of five objects
10 Tomás deTorquemada

## QUIZ 177

1 Peter Jackson
2 The Specials
3 *The Twilight Zone*
4 Rocky Marciano
5 1789
6 the Pacific
7 Dirty But Clean
8 the pumpkin
9 b) stinging
10 Australia

## QUIZ 179

1 W C Fields
2 Daphne and Celeste
3 Dobbin
4 Kapil Dev
5 Egypt
6 Krakatoa
7 Erewhon
8 the heart
9 b) the number 13
10 R

## QUIZ 176

1 *Working Girl*
2 Gloria Estefan
3 Galton and Simpson
4 Steve Davis
5 Liechtenstein
6 they lay eggs
7 Arthur Ransome
8 J M Barrie
9 b) weapon
10 between the ribs

## QUIZ 178

1 *Halloween III: Season of the Witch*
2 The Tremeloes
3 Michael Elphick
4 Cowdenbeath
5 Salem
6 carbon dioxide
7 Anne Rice
8 No Doubt
9 c) a layer of fine hair
10 Spain

## QUIZ 180

1 Sally Kellerman
2 Phil Collins
3 John Noakes
4 78
5 The Netherlands
6 San Francisco
7 Agatha Christie
8 Jack Nicholson
9 c) deceive
10 a hairstyle

# SOLUTIONS

## QUIZ 181

1. *Dune*
2. Atomic Kitten
3. John Goodman
4. fencing
5. 1918
6. wind velocity
7. Aphra Behn
8. Van Helsing
9. c) words
10. at Monte Carlo

## QUIZ 182

1. Michael Douglas
2. violin
3. Monkey
4. Edinburgh
5. Charles II
6. the liver
7. *Brick Lane*
8. Audrey Hepburn
9. b) knife
10. Joan of Arc

## QUIZ 183

1. Orson Welles
2. Dawn
3. *House*
4. Florence Griffith-Joyner
5. Christopher Columbus
6. the limpet
7. *Othello*
8. Sir Ian McKellen
9. b) elections
10. British Academy of Film and Television Arts

## QUIZ 184

1. *L A Confidential*
2. the Doobie Brothers
3. Leeds
4. Naples
5. Danish
6. a swan
7. *The Color Purple*
8. *Solaris*
9. b) a mistake
10. the Victoria Cross

## QUIZ 185

1. Joel and Ethan Coen
2. Fugees
3. Xena
4. Turin, Italy
5. Harold II
6. iron
7. Andrew Motion
8. Will Scarlet
9. b) an onion
10. wing commander

## QUIZ 186

1. Barbarella
2. the Big Bopper
3. Bobby Davro
4. 37
5. Italy
6. Pluto
7. Raymond Chandler
8. Britt Ekland
9. a) a spicy sauce
10. Theseus

# SOLUTIONS

## QUIZ 187

1. *His Girl Friday*
2. the piano
3. Colin Dexter
4. draughts
5. 1994
6. James Watt
7. Rembrandt
8. Ade Edmondson
9. c) fragrant
10. the Temple of Artemis

## QUIZ 188

1. Toto
2. Elmer Bernstein
3. *Porridge*
4. the marathon
5. Massachusetts
6. the periodic table
7. Bill Bryson
8. Chisholm
9. c) archery
10. North Atlantic Treaty Organization

## QUIZ 189

1. *Goldfinger*
2. six
3. *Wacky Races*
4. Washington
5. the Vietnam War
6. 90
7. Jonathan Swift
8. Tim Burton
9. c) a fish
10. Parker

## QUIZ 190

1. surfing
2. The Who
3. *The Flumps*
4. baseball
5. Edward the Confessor
6. Albert Einstein
7. Edgar Allan Poe
8. *The Lost Boys*
9. c) wagons
10. Oz

## QUIZ 191

1. none
2. the Banshees
3. six
4. 90m/100 yards
5. Australia
6. Sir Clive Sinclair
7. Kazuo Ishiguro
8. *Girl with a Pearl Earring*
9. b) everywhere
10. a coot

## QUIZ 192

1. *The Core*
2. Gene Pitney
3. Frankie Howerd
4. Everton
5. Queen Victoria
6. a monkey
7. Aslan
8. Jennifer Lopez
9. b) warlike
10. *Viz*

# SOLUTIONS

## QUIZ 193

1 *Amélie*
2 *Rigoletto*
3 Christopher Eccleston
4 32
5 Magna Carta
6 lead
7 Thomas Gainsborough
8 *A Midsummer Night's Dream*
9 c) sleep all summer
10 Errol Flynn

## QUIZ 194

1 Gary Oldman
2 Mark Knopfler
3 *The Big Breakfast*
4 tenpin bowling
5 Jimmy Carter
6 10,000
7 Christopher Brookmyre
8 *Rock Follies*
9 c) wear it
10 *The Times*

## QUIZ 195

1 the sinking of the *Titanic*
2 Antonín Dvořák
3 Doctor Who
4 Cluedo
5 the Incas
6 the hand
7 Dario Fo
8 *Wargames*
9 a) an instrument of torture
10 Hercules

## QUIZ 196

1 *Road to Perdition*
2 Fairground Attraction
3 Tony Hancock
4 the Cresta Run
5 the Pacific Ocean
6 the candela
7 Auguste Rodin
8 *The Jungle Book*
9 a) animal scales
10 tally-ho!

## QUIZ 197

1 *Heat*
2 Marvin Gaye
3 George Costanza
4 croquet
5 1776
6 the gallon
7 Sylvia Plath
8 *Cape Fear*
9 a) every five years
10 ivory

## QUIZ 198

1 *The Chronicles of Narnia: The Lion, the Witch and the Wardrobe*
2 Aaron Copland
3 Holby
4 chess
5 the Crimean War
6 Chernobyl
7 Henry Moore
8 Steve McQueen
9 a) a coin
10 a total eclipse

# SOLUTIONS

## QUIZ 199

1  *Invasion of the Bodysnatchers*
2  'Denis'
3  *Hawaii Five-0*
4  tennis
5  Pancho Villa
6  Uganda
7  P D James
8  owls
9  b) a medium-sized head
10 Cambridge

## QUIZ 200

1  Anton Karas
2  Roxette
3  *Surgical Spirit*
4  2000
5  Kenya
6  three
7  Euripides
8  *The Last Samurai*
9  c) caves
10 Wolfgang Amadeus Mozart

## QUIZ 201

1  John Cleese
2  Chas and Dave
3  Mark Thompson
4  Sebastian Coe
5  William Bligh
6  Panama
7  Clive Cussler
8  the thigh
9  a) fan-shaped
10 Nancy Astor

## QUIZ 202

1  Frank Capra
2  Barry Manilow
3  Gabriel
4  Sunderland
5  the Pacific
6  colours
7  *Life of Pi*
8  Lara Croft
9  b) in a bullfight
10 Goliath

## QUIZ 203

1  *Raiders of the Lost Ark*
2  Beard
3  *Pie in the Sky*
4  Emil Zatopek
5  Anthony Eden
6  Cyprus
7  Henry and Edward
8  India
9  c) blood pressure
10 Al Gore

## QUIZ 204

1  Sir Guy of Gisbourne
2  Stravinsky
3  Bouvier
4  James Hunt
5  Delaware
6  Uranus
7  Asperger's syndrome
8  Barb Wire
9  b) hairy
10 diphtheria

# SOLUTIONS

## QUIZ 205

1 *Donnie Brasco*
2 Sid Vicious
3 Sharon Gless
4 Moscow, USSR
5 St Andrews
6 the Lake District
7 Thomas Pynchon
8 Cilla Black
9 c) dark purple-red
10 Black Bess

## QUIZ 206

1 George Lucas
2 Rose Royce
3 *Magpie*
4 25
5 Israel
6 gannet
7 Florence
8 Ron Howard
9 c) an egg capsule
10 Paris

## QUIZ 207

1 Jennifer Saunders
2 Bruce Spingsteen
3 It's That Man Again
4 four
5 Douglas
6 laughing gas
7 Luis Buñuel
8 Evelyn Waugh
9 c) mercenary
10 Swedish

## QUIZ 208

1 *Casino*
2 Stephen Sondheim
3 $6 million
4 Willie Carson
5 Jacobites
6 O, A, B, AB
7 Barbara Hepworth
8 Poison Ivy
9 b) foul
10 iceberg

## QUIZ 209

1 Frankenstein
2 Toto
3 Connie Booth
4 Amsterdam
5 Cyprus
6 Alva
7 Andy Warhol
8 Ant McPartlin
9 b) a jury
10 Barbie®

## QUIZ 210

1 *Alien*
2 'Boys'
3 Bamber Gascoigne
4 baize
5 Israel
6 Piltdown Man
7 *Crime and Punishment*
8 *Cal*
9 a) courage
10 Thursday

# SOLUTIONS

## QUIZ 211

1  Galadriel
2  The Byrds
3  Jim Davidson
4  cycling
5  Port of Spain
6  a newt
7  David Herbert
8  *Bedazzled*
9  c) lamplight
10 Shinto

## QUIZ 212

1  Roger Daltrey
2  *The Guns of Navarone*
3  *Game On!*
4  motorcycle speedway
5  Davy Crockett
6  the bumblebee
7  Ansel Adams
8  George Michael
9  a) torture
10 a polar bear

## QUIZ 213

1  Edward G Robinson
2  Ennio Morricone
3  Grizzly Adams
4  seven
5  New Zealand
6  penicillin
7  Glasgow
8  *Intolerable Cruelty*
9  b) reptiles
10 Indiana

## QUIZ 214

1  the Scarecrow
2  Manic Street Preachers
3  Michael Grade
4  Sir Robin Knox-Johnston
5  Malawi
6  the blackberry and the raspberry
7  *A Midsummer Night's Dream*
8  *Original Sin*
9  c) the elbow
10 the camel

## QUIZ 215

1  Fred Astaire
2  Eighth Wonder
3  BBC Radio 2
4  1992
5  Alexander the Great
6  1/12
7  Dr Watson
8  *The Misfits*
9  c) luxury
10 Jimmy Savile

## QUIZ 216

1  Bruce Lee
2  Ricky Martin
3  Felicity Scully
4  1984
5  Somalia
6  grapefruit
7  Giotto
8  *Young Adam*
9  a) skirt
10 Frances Hodgson Burnett

# SOLUTIONS

## QUIZ 217

1 *Three Colours Blue*
2 Donna Summer
3 the Terrahawks
4 Frankie Dettori
5 1956
6 Saturn's rings
7 John Masefield
8 Hole
9 b) proper names
10 Juliet

## QUIZ 218

1 Laurence Olivier
2 'N Sync
3 Dill
4 Italy
5 Luddites
6 carbon
7 James Herriot
8 *Voice of an Angel*
9 b) a beggar
10 two

## QUIZ 219

1 Owen Wilson
2 John Kettley
3 Lenny Henry
4 darts
5 Claudius
6 Colorado
7 the Beats
8 Gordon Ramsay
9 b) between rulers
10 Elmer Fudd

## QUIZ 220

1 Lauren Bacall
2 The Wurzels
3 Catweazle
4 Desert Orchid
5 Genghis Khan
6 a grasshopper-like insect
7 Charles Dickens
8 Daisy Duke
9 b) a shrewish woman
10 2 February

## QUIZ 221

1 *Out of Sight*
2 *Octopussy*
3 *Beverly Hills 90210*
4 Fulham
5 1979
6 John and W K Kellogg
7 John Steinbeck
8 the Fabulous Baker Boys
9 b) a plant
10 Margaret Thatcher

## QUIZ 222

1 *A Few Good Men*
2 Dizzy
3 David Cassidy
4 West Germany
5 Uzbekistan
6 eel
7 *Pride and Prejudice*
8 Keith Richards
9 c) French
10 Vulcan

# SOLUTIONS

## QUIZ 223

1  *The Day the Earth Stood Still*
2  *Back to the Future*
3  Mickey Dolenz
4  Munro-bagging
5  Honduras
6  Bill Gates
7  Henrik Ibsen
8  'Fallin''
9  b) curse
10  five euros

## QUIZ 224

1  a leopard
2  Irene Cara
3  *Treasure Hunt*
4  aikido
5  Japan
6  potatoes
7  George Eliot
8  *The Bill*
9  c) using abusive language
10  The Mamas and The Papas

## QUIZ 225

1  Steve Martin
2  *Evita*
3  *Family Guy*
4  seven-and-a-half minutes
5  Dr Samuel Johnson
6  the ear
7  *The 39 Steps*
8  Aaron
9  b) extinct cattle
10  *Coronation Street*

## QUIZ 226

1  a rabbit
2  Bachman-Turner Overdrive
3  *The House of Eliott*
4  the caber
5  Berserkers
6  the ohm
7  Dorothy L Sayers
8  a lawyer
9  c) short
10  dreams

## QUIZ 227

1  rosebud
2  Miles Davis
3  *The Brittas Empire*
4  kendo
5  Berne
6  green
7  Michelangelo
8  Joan of Arc
9  a) a killer whale
10  Sylvester

## QUIZ 228

1  Supergirl
2  Gilbert and Sullivan
3  *Bewitched*
4  red
5  Mali
6  beriberi
7  Edgar Allan Poe
8  Francis Ford Coppola
9  a) an introduction
10  Tin Pan Alley

# SOLUTIONS

## QUIZ 229

1 Al Jolson
2 Tony Christie
3 Leo McKern
4 Duncan Goodhew
5 Italy
6 sulphur
7 Donna Tartt
8 *Hitch*
9 a) furnishing
10 Icarus

## QUIZ 230

1 Bruce Willis
2 Guns 'N' Roses
3 helicopters
4 Allan Border
5 Caracas
6 the foot
7 the Turner Prize
8 *Will and Grace*
9 c) uprooted
10 Czech

## QUIZ 231

1 Burt Lancaster
2 the crotchet
3 *The West Wing*
4 golf
5 Spencer Perceval
6 grape
7 *Pequod*
8 *Ronin*
9 c) play it
10 Mephistopheles

## QUIZ 232

1 *Once Upon a Time in the West*
2 guitar
3 Pierce Brosnan
4 Preston
5 1929
6 courgette
7 *The Tempest*
8 *LA Law*
9 a) water in a lake
10 Victoria

## QUIZ 233

1 Will Smith
2 saxophone
3 *The Invaders*
4 the Green Bay Packers
5 Staffa
6 the triceps
7 Mrs Pepperpot
8 *Legally Blonde*
9 c) an aromatic plant
10 May

## QUIZ 234

1 Utah
2 Paul Robeson
3 Tanya Turner
4 Michel Platini
5 Cyprus
6 birds
7 Dan Brown
8 *Legend*
9 b) an idiot
10 pears

# SOLUTIONS

## QUIZ 235

1 *Reign of Fire*
2 Puccini
3 *100%*
4 Jimmy Armfield
5 Pakistan
6 ten
7 Enid Blyton
8 'Love and Kisses'
9 a) a storm
10 John

## QUIZ 236

1 *Beetlejuice*
2 Wolfgang Amadeus Mozart
3 *Tiswas*
4 Lillehammer, Norway
5 Colchester
6 worms
7 *Far From the Madding Crowd*
8 Gloria Hunniford
9 c) a manuscript
10 Pyotr Ilyich Tchaikovsky

## QUIZ 237

1 Nigel Bruce
2 Flanders and Swann
3 Leadbetter
4 ice
5 the right
6 hummingbird
7 Charlie Higson
8 *The Amityville Horror*
9 c) long-winded
10 feng shui

## QUIZ 238

1 *The Conversation*
2 Destiny's Child
3 Dr Quinn
4 twelve
5 Edinburgh
6 the brain
7 photography
8 *The Stepford Wives*
9 a) sleight of hand
10 a rat

## QUIZ 239

1 The Beatles
2 Jethro Tull
3 Alec Guinness
4 coursing
5 Mao Zedong
6 Mauritius
7 James Joyce
8 Rose Tyler
9 c) a letter of the alphabet
10 the banshee

## QUIZ 240

1 E Annie Proulx
2 'Are 'Friends' Electric?'
3 Humphrey Lyttelton
4 Alain Prost
5 Lisbon
6 Proxima Centauri
7 Theodore Géricault
8 her face
9 c) a net
10 Captain Haddock

# SOLUTIONS

## QUIZ 241

1 Claude Rains
2 Billy Ray Cyrus
3 *The Love Boat*
4 Jean-Marc Bosman
5 Nigeria
6 James Lovelock
7 rats
8 Sir Patrick Moore
9 b) evening
10 Umberto Eco

## QUIZ 242

1 John Carpenter
2 Vanilla
3 *Red Dwarf*
4 Jackie Stewart
5 Mauritius
6 Laika
7 Arthur Koestler
8 Donatella Versace
9 c) finger
10 The Philippines

## QUIZ 243

1 *ER*
2 The Tremeloes
3 *Love Thy Neighbour*
4 Joey Dunlop
5 Bombay
6 blood circulation
7 *Digital Fortress*
8 *Kingdom of Heaven*
9 b) a leaf stalk
10 blue ribbon

## QUIZ 244

1 *Alien Resurrection*
2 Queen
3 Stephen Fry
4 the main body of riders in a race
5 French
6 the wren
7 Ian Fleming
8 Sarah Brightman
9 a) to stop
10 Philip

## QUIZ 245

1 The Band
2 Thompson Twins
3 *Playschool*
4 the pole vault
5 Harold Wilson
6 an unkindness
7 Henri de Toulouse-Lautrec
8 Velma
9 b) a hard outer coating
10 Doris Day

## QUIZ 246

1 Johnny Weissmuller
2 Barry Manilow
3 *Listen with Mother*
4 50
5 Sicily
6 the Plough
7 Cookham, Berkshire
8 Debbie Reynolds
9 c) a man whose wife has been unfaithful
10 the antelope

# SOLUTIONS

## QUIZ 247

1 *The Cook, The Thief, His Wife and Her Lover*
2 Astrud Gilberto
3 Chris Evans
4 1981
5 T'aipei
6 32
7 Raphael
8 Rick Stein
9 a) goosebumps
10 eight

## QUIZ 248

1 John Wayne
2 The Kinks
3 *The Good Old Days*
4 Miguel Indurain
5 the Vatican
6 Antony Gormley
7 the orchid
8 Mexican
9 c) the sound of wind in one's intestines
10 E

## QUIZ 249

1 Dopey
2 Johann Sebastian Bach
3 Dame Maggie Smith
4 water polo
5 Saudi Arabia
6 tuberculosis
7 Fauvism
8 Jane Russell
9 b) by making lengthy speeches
10 rum and lime juice

## QUIZ 250

1 *The Sound of Music*
2 Michael Nyman
3 Mr Benn
4 hot air ballooning
5 Andorra
6 1978
7 the Uffizi, Florence
8 Delia Smith
9 a) a redhead
10 Lebanon